awakening your
PSYCHIC SKILLS

awakening your
PSYCHIC SKILLS

using intuition to guide your life

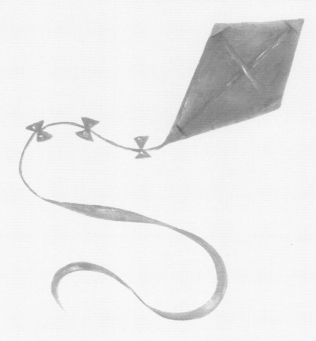

JOANNE E. BRUNN

First edition for North America published in 2004 by
Barron's Educational Series, Inc.

First published in Great Britain in 2004 by
Godsfield, a division of Octopus Publishing
Group Ltd 2004

Project Editor: Emily Casey Bailey
Project Designer: Lisa McCormick
Illustrator: Kim Glass
Page Makeup: Kevin Knight

Designed and produced for Octopus Publishing Group Ltd by
The Bridgewater Book Company

All inquiries should be addressed to:
Barron's Educational Series, Inc.
250 Wireless Boulevard
Hauppauge, New York 11788
http://www.barronseduc.com

International Standard Book Number 0-7641-2714-4
Library of Congress Catalog Card Number 2003106920

Printed and bound in China

9 8 7 6 5 4 3 2 1

Author dedication

To my husband, Lou Veltri, for his ever-present physical and spiritual sustenance.

To my higher self and the knowings of the collective unconscious for support on my journey.

To Brenda Rosen and especially David Bolitho for recognizing my practical psychic nature.

To my friends for sharing their stories.

Contents

Introduction

Everyone has psychic skills. When you're faced with a difficult decision or need information to help you understand what's going on, there's no need to telephone the psychic hotline. As you'll discover, with a little practice, you can be your own psychic advisor!

Being psychic is about being sensitive, perceptive, and understanding; it is a potent form of inner wisdom. I'm sure you've had times when your instincts were on high alert. Perhaps you had a hunch that there would be a certain outcome, a gut feeling that you should take one action instead of another, a dream that gave you needed information, or a flash of recognition that something about a situation was familiar. You use your intuition every day in ordinary situations, ranging from what you feel like having for dinner, or what movie you feel like seeing, to major decisions such as looking for a job or relocating. These feelings come from the deep intuitive knowledge we all have—our psychic selves.

If you doubt that you are naturally psychic, think back to how you looked at the world when you were a child. Young children have not yet learned to block their nonphysical perceptions. As a result, they are more viscerally aware of connections and meaningful coincidences. They have permission from society to imagine, dream, and fantasize. They often have imaginary playmates, which in many cultures are an accepted part of the belief system in the form of spirit guides or animal helpers.

Children often see colors around people—auras or fields of energy that help them to figure out their moods. Babies and animals have an intuitive sense of who to trust. They often gravitate to certain people because they sense that they can get what they need from them at that particular time. Even older children often know what younger children want before they can speak or verbalize their thoughts.

Many animals also exhibit psychic behavior. Dogs are remarkably telepathic and respond to unspoken commands. They may come into the room when you have only been thinking about taking them for a walk, and know that you are preparing to leave even before you put on your coat or pick up your keys. Dog trainers observe that it is impossible to fool your dog by thinking one thing and saying another. Pets often try to console you when you are upset and may lead you somewhere or make you leave a place when they sense danger. They may take an instant dislike to a stranger, similar to the way children do, perhaps because that person is not trustworthy or sincere. My dog used to wait in anticipation at the front door for my mother to come home. Even though she had an erratic work schedule, he always knew when to station himself there.

There are many stories of animals fleeing an area a day or two before an earthquake. In Japan, many people keep goldfish because it is said they become agitated and behave abnormally before an eruption. Animals are often able to find their way home over long distances without relying on memory or sense of smell to guide them back.

For ancient cultures (and those peoples who still practice traditional ways), connection to the spirit world or dream states was a part of everyday life. They commonly practiced divination to predict the future. In ancient Mesopotamia, the future was predicted from such things as the intestines of slaughtered animals, fire and smoke, the sounds of springs, and the shapes of plants. They

No matter how unpredictable a homecoming may be, dogs often know when their owners are approaching.

found meanings in all of nature. The people of ancient China practiced divination by burning a bone or tortoiseshell upon which questions had been engraved. The answers were read in the patterns of cracks caused by the heat. Until the recent Chinese takeover of Tibet, many people were practicing divinators. In Africa, many tribes use cowrie shells to predict future events or to ask questions of the universe. The toothed side of the shell signifies a "yes" response. The number that lands toothed side up versus the total number thrown determines the probability of the future event. Even the art of many cultures, such as rock and bark paintings and ritual masks, shows a connection to other worlds.

What Is Intuition?

Intuition should not be thought of as mysterious or part of the occult, although many people believe or promote the idea that being psychic is strange or even malevolent. Edgar Cayce (1877–1945), one of the greatest Western psychics, felt that being psychic was an extension of our own conscious and unconscious minds and should be thought of as a natural process.

Albert Schweitzer (1875–1965), Alsatian-German theologian, philosopher, musician, and mission doctor, felt that in order to live a deeper reality, one had to experience extraordinary perception. Even the noted Viennese founder of psychoanalysis, Sigmund Freud (1856–1939), stated that in retrospect he would have studied psychical research rather than psychoanalysis.

Where is this place of deeper reality where your true potential lies? That place might be called your unconscious, your intuition, your higher self, or your *daimon*—a term used by the Greeks to define your soul-companion, the carrier of your destiny, your potential.

The place where you connect with your intuition is known by many names. William Blake (1757–1827), English poet, painter, and visionary mystic, called it the *divine imagination*. The American psychologist and Jungian analyst James Hillman refers to it as the *imaginal realm*. To the ancient Greek philosopher Plato, this was where the ideal

You are open to the collective arena of ideas, images, thoughts, and knowings.

archetypes lived. The Australian aborigines refer to this rich and complex spirituality as the *dreamtime*. The Sufis call it *alam al-mithal*. The Tibetans call it the *sambhogakaya*—the dimension of inner richness. The Swiss psychologist and psychiatrist Carl Jung (1875–1961) knew this realm as the *collective symbolic unconscious*—that which is inherited from the ancestors.

This is the place where all information is available for the asking. Did you ever feel that you were a part of something much larger and greater than your local, physical self? Have you ever had the sense of being connected with all beings? This state is often called *flow*, which has been defined as a feeling of an almost automatic, effortless, highly focused state of consciousness. When in that state, you are open to the collective arena of ideas, images, thoughts, and knowings that flow into you in an almost endless stream.

You could enter this state unconsciously or consciously through athletics, art, dance, music, or being with a loved one. Edgar Cayce felt that meditation was the best conscious way in which to open your psychic abilities. During a meditation, a visualization, or perhaps an activity where you reach a high-flow state, images, symbols, sounds, or feelings will appear to you. These are clues to your most important feelings, solutions to problems, or to a helper on your journey.

Because images and feelings are often symbolic and fragmented, they will not make sense to your rational mind. Instead of dismissing these psychic indicators, as most people do, bring this intuitive information into your conscious mind so that you can interpret it. The symbols and feelings can then be combined with other rational data and used to make decisions to create powerful and effective guidelines for living.

Intuition contains the codes for health, happiness, and the survival of all good things on this planet. Intuition exists inside all of us. Its language consists of symbols, metaphors, silence, sounds, energy, feelings, and knowings. It is a language that most people have forgotten, but it is your first language—you can recapture it and learn to use it every day, if you want.

Why Develop This Language?

In the seventeenth century, the sciences of physics, astronomy, chemistry, and medicine began to emerge. This devotion to a mechanistic world began to suffocate the sense of individual belonging and connection to the universe. As a result, anything that could not be reduced to scientific study and measured, such as creativity, intuition, and consciousness, was relegated to the status of superstition. Human nature was redefined as physical, and science discouraged us from looking within ourselves for meanings. The attitude of mechanistic science proclaims the inability of humans to attain and grasp the truth. In this world view, telepathy, precognition, psychokinesis, and all other forms of what science calls parapsychological events were deemed impossible. The notions of synchronicity and coincidences were reduced to the mathematics of probability and were trivialized. The world became cause and effect, black and white.

Even today, we are taught in schools and by society that physical intelligence is more important than spiritual knowledge and intuition. Because of this mechanistic predilection, high value is placed on the kinds of knowledge that promote and contribute to further mechanical technologies. The natural, intuitive sense we took for granted as children diminishes, because this sixth sense is not valued or accepted like the five "regular" senses. Rational thinking, logic, and intelligence are the only roads to success and accomplishment.

This mechanistic emphasis often starts in schools when spontaneity is controlled and the ability to freely associate ideas is stifled. When rules are unyielding and learning structures are too rigid, there is no room for growth and exploration. Creativity, a necessary element of psychic ability, cannot thrive in these environments. When teachers ridicule unusual ideas and do not tolerate a playful attitude, creativity suffers and intuition subsequently shuts down.

Shutting down our intuitive senses leads to various problems. Life becomes mysterious and confusing, and we often have a difficult time making choices or figuring out what to do.

Schools teach that intelligence is more important than intuition.

Fortunately, intuition is so ingrained in the psyche that it can be buried but not destroyed. With a bit of effort, you can recapture the inner sources of help and guidance you knew as a child. When you begin to trust your intuition and your innate psychic skills, life becomes easier and more fun. Indeed, your psychic ability can enhance virtually every aspect of your life, providing you with a deeper and richer understanding of your life and your unique purpose.

When you recapture your intuitive and psychic abilities, you will have the practical benefit of finding yourself in the right place at the right time all of the time. You will consistently find synchronicities and coincidences happening. Trains and buses will appear when you need them. Waiting in line at the post office and grocery store will be a thing of the past. You will intuitively know which road to take to avoid traffic jams. Your ability to solve problems and make better decisions will improve. You will gain self-esteem and confidence. In many cases, you will know how to handle your own matters instead of handing control over to the experts in the fields of medicine, law, and mechanics, to name a few.

Look around you. The most successful and happy people are often very intuitive; consciously or unconsciously, they have learned to trust their hunches and notice synchronicities and other messages from the nonphysical world. Because they have learned to live in tune with their internal rhythms, their creativity blossoms, and they manifest more of their innate potential.

When your intuitive channel is open, you begin to function at a higher level of awareness. You can see distractions and problems of everyday life for what they are—minor issues. In this state of awareness, you can explore telepathy (mind-to-mind communication) and precognition (awareness of future events). You have a higher probability of better personal health, more balanced emotions, and a sense of inner peace. This overall well-being allows you to think more clearly and live life with boundless energy—energy that comes from your focus on higher states instead of being used up worrying about little things or twisted up in fear or anger.

Opening up to intuition causes powerful results, both for you personally and for those with whom you interact. It is important to ensure that these results are positive and are intended for the highest good. Therefore, before entering into any meditation, visualization, or grounding in preparation for accessing your innate psychic abilities, ask your deities, spirit guides, or highest self for guidance and wisdom in using the information that you receive in the most respectful and appropriate manner. This way you can feel comfortable that the information you use or share with someone will be relevant, necessary, and useful.

What You Will Learn

The simple exercises and techniques in this book can help you in many practical ways you can use every day. You'll learn to:

✳ use inner guidance to answer questions or make decisions

✳ gain an advantage at work or make your work tasks easier

✳ deepen and improve relationships with lovers, friends, children, and family

✳ avoid traffic jams and dangers while traveling

✳ use energy to heal yourself and to send healing to others

✳ use your dreams to solve problems or bring clarity to a confusing situation

✳ awaken your creativity and discover hidden talents

✳ see into your future.

As you explore the techniques in this book, your awareness will increase. Awakening your psychic skills can help you live more fully and deeply, in touch with who you are and in tune with the natural rhythms that guide our world.

An overall feeling of well-being affords you the probability of inner peace.

CHAPTER ONE *You may use words other than* psychic *to express your intuitive nature, because the word has many negative and amusing connotations. Think about the times you have said, "I was flying by the seat of my pants," "We were on the same wavelength," or "I could really feel the vibes." What you were really saying is that you were tuned into your psychic gifts.*

How Psychic Am I?

A "psychic advisor" is often pictured as an old woman in colorful clothes and a head scarf, dripping with costume jewelry, reading cards behind a curtain at the back of a shabby storefront. The unseen person on the other side of the psychic hotline, on the other hand, is visualized as a needy college student reading from a script about issues that are so general they could apply to anyone.

These stereotypes limit our willingness to explore our psychic gifts. Nowadays, many psychic advisors are more like counselors or therapists—ordinary people who have honed their intuitive skills so that they can suggest advice and offer valuable insights. Some psychic advisors, called medical intuitives, specialize in diagnosing puzzling medical conditions, often without ever meeting the patient. Others help police investigators find missing people or locate stolen property.

Even if you think there is not an intuitive bone in your body, you will learn that you are more psychic than you think you are. You will discover that situations or synchronicities that you dismissed as probabilities or mere coincidences were signs that your intuitive nature was struggling to be heard.

Test Your Psychic Ability

The first step is to recognize how often you already use your innate psychic gifts. Ask yourself the following questions. You may discover that you're already a practicing psychic.

✳ Have you ever finished the sentence of your lover, spouse, or friend?

✳ Have you ever walked into a house or apartment that you were thinking of buying or renting and found that it immediately just "felt right" or made you feel uncomfortable?

✳ Do you sometimes know who is on the phone before you answer it?

✳ Have you ever smelled perfume or food cooking, or heard footsteps, in a place where someone has recently died?

✳ Have you ever entered a room after two people have been fighting and felt the tension, even if they were acting civil to each other and smiling?

✳ When your child is sick, do you intuitively know whether he or she needs to see a doctor or just needs to get some bed rest?

✳ Have you ever been engaged in an activity or visited a new place and experienced a sense of déjà vu—the feeling that you have done something before in exactly the same way, or that you have been to a particular place before?

✳ Have you ever gone on a job interview and known you were going to get the job even though you may not have had the exact qualifications for it?

✳ Have you ever had a premonition dream—in other words, have you ever dreamed of something that then happened?

✳ Have you ever been driving and had a feeling that the car next to you was about to pull in front of you—and then it did?

✳ When you were young, did you sometimes get the feeling that your mother wanted you to come home—and she did?

Practice: Psychic Games

The following games are fun to play with a group of friends. You may be surprised at how psychic you all are!

✴ Have a friend put an object in a bag. Without touching the bag, think about your impressions of what it contains. Is the object hard or soft? What does it smell or taste like? What might it be used for?

✴ Have a friend draw a picture in another room. Think about the picture—what are your impressions of the subject matter? Is it a picture of a particular place? Do you feel hot or cold there? What types of activities might occur there?

✴ Have one friend pick a room in the house to physically go into and choose where in the room to sit, stand, or lie down. Your friend might also choose to hold an object in the room or face a particular direction. Try to feel the environment where your friend is. What color are the walls? What is the room used for?

Many of the events that you might have ignored or regarded as simple everyday occurrences are demonstrations of your psychic ability. Being aware of psychic occurrences and playing the sort of games mentioned above, from guessing who is on the phone to reading a friend's mind, will begin to convince you of your own innate intuitive skills while opening up your psychic channels. These exercises are not "games" in the frivolous or superficial sense, but are activities that also happen to be fun and that are designed to make you feel more comfortable with exploring your long-buried innate abilities. As you begin to practice these skills more seriously, you need to consider the consequences of your actions. Edgar Cayce talked about the importance of opening to the power of unconditional love as we practice our skills. Entering all exercises with love and the intention of the highest good for all involved will ensure that the outcome is appropriate.

Do you sometimes know who is on the phone before you answer it?

Awaken Your Inner Psychic

Everyone has psychic skills, but they may have become rusty with disuse. You would not expect to play a great game of tennis if it's been years since you swung a racket, or to cook a gourmet meal if you've been eating out every evening. Neither can you expect to be instantly adept at using your psychic abilities if you have not practiced them for a while.

Of course, some people have stronger innate psychic abilities than others, just as some people make better cooks or tennis players. Like all skills, psychic gifts have much to do with how much you enjoy the activity and how strongly you desire to excel. Research studies conducted in the 1930s to prove the existence of telepathy using ESP cards found that people who were motivated to do well and believed that telepathy was possible scored higher than average. Thus, believing in yourself and in your own powers of deep intuition is essential to tuning up your psychic skills.

Think about your intuition as getting to know a new friend. Communicate, spend time together, talk, listen, and get to know each other. Talk and listen for the response when you are walking, commuting to work, riding your bicycle, taking a shower, or working around the house. I find I can best quiet my rational mind when I am driving my car. Living near New York City, it is imperative to be fully aware of everything going on around me on the road—front, back, and sideways! While my left brain is completely engaged with all the busy work of following the rules of the road and paying attention to the other drivers, it does not interfere with my right brain, which is asking questions and receiving responses from the Universe.

One of the best ways to reawaken your dormant skills is through meditation. As the meditative state deepens, synchronistic coincidences occur more frequently. Prayer can also have similar effects. Whether you repeat a mantra, say a prayer, chant, or follow your breathing, you will be led to experience a holistic view of yourself and the world. This reawakening also has a spiritual component. Your meditation or prayer practice can help you to form a closer connection with your deities, spirit guides, or higher self, who provide guidance in channeling your techniques for the highest good.

Meditation physically balances the right and left hemispheres of the brain. The EEG activity of each hemisphere actually mirrors that of the other in terms of frequency and correlation of wave activity. Trance dancing and drumming are other activities that have been shown to balance the brain's hemispheres. When these practices are performed consistently with dedication and high intent, you will become more balanced physically, mentally, emotionally, and spiritually. This completely balanced state is optimal for opening receptivity to intuitive insights. As you practice the skills, you will find it easier to quickly calm your mind when you need to tap into that psychic place. A regular practice of meditation, chanting, drumming, or trance dance will provide the structure and discipline needed to reawaken and further develop your innate psychic skills.

The balanced state of meditation is optimal for opening receptivity to intuitive insights.

Methods of Meditation

Meditation is the simple, but not necessarily easy, act of quieting your mind. In traditional meditation, you need to quiet both your body and mind. However, you may find that you can also quiet your mind by running, dancing, walking through a forest, or listening to music. Honor your own method of meditation, because you intuitively know what works for you. It is important to be consistent and meditate every day at the same time. Fifteen minutes of quiet sitting or a morning walk is all it takes. Your objective is to enter a light trance, the place of being partially awake and partially asleep, similar to the feeling you have upon awakening in the morning. Your present surroundings will fade into the background as you enter a peaceful state of consciousness.

In order to quiet your mind, whether you are sitting still or engaged in a physical activity, you can choose to repeat your own affirmations. For example, "I am a deeply intuitive person. I am in tune with the Universe." Repeating a chant or a mantra will help raise your energy to a higher vibration. "*Om Mani Padme Hum*" is the most widely used of all Buddhist mantras. It cannot easily be translated into a simple phrase because it is said that all the teachings of the Buddha are contained in this mantra.

I often start my sitting meditations with alternate-nostril breathing. This type of yogic breathing brings fresh energy to both hemispheres of the brain. *Yogis*, devoted practitioners of yoga, consider this the best technique to calm the mind and the nervous system. Most of us do not breathe equally with both nostrils. You may notice that one side is easier to breathe through than the other at various times throughout the day. Because we need energy in both sides of our brains for optimum intuitive and analytic functions, this technique ensures a balance. The yogis believe that the breath monitors *prana*, also known as *chi*—the life-force energy in the body. Research studies have shown that people did better on creative tests when their left nostril was clearer, bringing more air and energy to the right side of the brain. Similarly, people did better with analytic tests when their right nostril was clearer.

Practice: Alternate-Nostril Breathing

It is easy and relaxing to do alternate-nostril breathing. Each time you return to the point at which you started is one round. Start with three rounds and add more as you are comfortable. Be sure to breathe slowly and without any strain.

1 Close your right nostril with your right thumb, and breathe out through the left nostril. Slowly exhale as much air as possible.

2 Slowly breathe in through your left nostril. Take as deep a breath as possible.

3 Close your left nostril with your right ring finger (or any finger that is comfortable for you) and remove your thumb from your right nostril. Breathe out through your right nostril. Empty the lungs as much as possible.

4 Slowly begin to inhale through the same (right) nostril.

5 Now alternate nostrils again. Close off the right nostril with the thumb, and breathe out through the left, just as you did in the beginning.

6 Continue to breathe in and out through alternate nostrils.

7 When you are finished, take a few deep slow breaths through both nostrils. Allow the breath to return to normal.

Alternate-nostril breathing brings fresh energy to both sides of the brain.

Listening to Your Inner Self

Another method for developing our intuition is simply to trust our inner selves. Intuition can be thought of as an information-gathering exercise for gaining elements of the truth. If you begin with small decisions, you will gradually trust your inner voice as much as your analytic mind. Allow images and symbols to simply arise instead of struggling to figure out the answer. Because intuition is innate, you don't have to try to receive impressions—just be open to their existence. You will make mistakes at first as you begin to distinguish the voices of your true inner self from all the other voices in your head. Making mistakes is important because you will learn the difference between an accurate intuitive impression versus one that comes in through your analytic mind and is based on fear, anger, or pure logic. If you feel nothing is happening—make it up! Pretend! Often, your guesses are accurate—why did you make that up instead of something else? Trust your inner self to "make up" the right impression.

Pay close attention to impressions that come just as you are falling asleep and just as you awaken.

One way to trust your inner self and quiet your rational mind is to be childlike and pretend that all things have meaning. Children are experts at make-believe and pretend

Practice: Making a Start

Practice first with everyday things. Should you take a different route to work? Where should you take your afternoon walk? When would be the best time to go to the bank? What is a good time to call your friend for a quick chat? Children learning to walk and talk start with small steps while they hold on to things and speak in simple sentences. Similarly, start with small steps and simple questions while uncovering how your intuition speaks to you. As you gain confidence in developing your skill, you can ask bigger and more important questions. Don't be afraid to fall and make mistakes. Be confident in your abilities. Soon you will be running and jumping!

play. Tap into that sleeping child within you. Through your intuition you have access to all the answers, but you need to know what questions to ask. When you pretend that your intuition can answer any question put to it, eventually you will gain the confidence that you have received the correct answers from the validating external feedback.

It is also important to pay close attention to impressions that come just as you are falling asleep and just as you awaken. Intuitive impressions are easily recognized at these times, when the boundaries between the waking and sleeping worlds are thin. Perhaps you already spend a few seconds or even minutes not quite certain if you are awake or asleep. Judgment seems to be suspended at these times, and engaging in rational thought is difficult. Take advantage of this in-between state by keeping a journal near your bed to record feelings and knowings that might help to clarify a current situation. You can also consciously create this state by taking a short nap when you need help with an issue. By entering a light sleep state with a conscious intention, your intuitive brain has the time to work on the issue without too much noise from the rational side. When you awaken, stay quiet and still and see what thoughts and feelings arise.

Practice: Focus for the Day

First thing in the morning, while you are still lying in bed and before you are fully awake, ask your inner self about your day. Hold the intention that any information you receive is for the highest good for yourself and all others involved in the situation. Is there anything you should or shouldn't do? What should you focus on today? Is there something you have been postponing that you need to take care of? If there is a situation that you have been confused about, now is the time to ask for some clarity. Let any feelings or knowings arise. You may get inspired to call up an old friend or ask your boss for more responsibility and a more senior position. Your intuition may be telling you that today is the perfect day for positive results.

Creativity and Intuition

Waking up your creativity is a fun and easy way to develop your intuition. When you express your creativity, you are naturally exercising your imagination. So go ahead and start doing all those things you didn't think you had time to do or that you thought were unimportant. Paint, dance, play an instrument, cook, write poetry, or garden. The intention to be creative is more important than what you do or how society might judge the task or the outcome. While in this creative frame of mind, the analytic nature is relaxed, allowing the intuitive flow to surface.

In many traditional cultures, there is no word for art or creativity, yet artistic expressions and creative endeavors are an accepted and necessary part of their everyday life. There is no mystery to being creative, because everyone is. What if in our own culture we were told that we were all artists, all creative beings? Imagine the possibilities when we are not afraid to excel, but encouraged to excel.

Fear, anger, and hostility often prevent us from opening up to this state. Loud inner critics interrupt our thoughts and discourage the use of our intuitive mind. The voices of family, friends, society, religious organizations, bosses, teachers, and the government consciously or unconsciously stop us from honoring our intuition. They say things like, "It doesn't make sense," "Prove it," "You can't just make things up," or "That's unrealistic." This causes your mind to label your intuitive thoughts as interference or imagination, and subsequently you disregard any information that is trying to come through.

I believe that everyone is creative, and that those people who have forgotten their creativity can be taught. My creative experiences have been engrossing, fun, and certainly expansive. Both creativity and the intuitive state can be defined as a state of heightened consciousness. Begin to think of yourself as a creative person and intuition will follow.

Practice: Creative Date

Make a date with yourself to be creative every day or at least once a week. Spend the time doing whatever activity makes you feel happiest. If you dreamed all week about flying a kite—go fly that kite! Take that art class or just go out into the woods and sketch. Spend all day Sunday playing with assorted spices, creating delectable foods. Have fun! You will discover that the time you spend giving yourself to creative pursuits reaps exponential rewards, increasing your intuition which, in turn, allows your life to run smoother. Your overall analytic skills will sharpen as you bring both sides of your brain into harmony.

Have fun! Allow yourself the time to go fly that kite.

Divination

One of the best ways to prove to yourself that your intuition truly does exist is with the help of divination tools. Some of these tools—such as tarot cards, numerology, muscle testing, the I-Ching, *and runes—will be presented in this book to whet your appetite in finding your favorite.*

Divination is the art or technique of determining the hidden significance or cause of events or the ability to predict the future by means of observing and interpreting signs. Ancient Romans used to believe that divination was concerned with uncovering the will of the gods. Today, divination is usually concerned with practical problems and is found in most cultures.

There are literally dozens of objects or events that serve as media of divination in various cultures. These include:

Different cultures use various items for divination, such as cowrie shells and tea leaves.

* crystals
* tarot cards
* tea leaves
* cowrie shells
* pendulums
* numbers
* I-Ching coins
* rune stones
* dowsing sticks

I have seen a Mongolian-Buryat shaman use a (full) vodka bottle to divine information about a person's health and current social situation. I have also witnessed a number of shamans from the Quechua tribe of Ecuador's high Andes use a candle for divination.

They rub it over a person's body, light the candle, and read the flame to ascertain the person's general health, determine areas that need attention, and divine the future.

Think of childhood fairy tales in which one of the characters gazed into a crystal ball, or a calm lake or a mirror. "Mirror, mirror, on the wall. . . ." Although we may find these images amusing, the technique of scrying has been used for hundreds of years in many cultures, and has even found its way into fairy tales. The term *scrying* comes from the English word *descry*, which means "to make out faintly" or "to reveal." Nostradamus practiced scrying by placing a lit candle next to a bowl of water. Staring into the water's surface revealed to him visions of people and events throughout the twenty-first century.

A dowsing stick is a searching tool that has been used for thousands of years to, most notably, locate underground water.

There are many methods of divination. Find one or a few that appeal to you, and practice their techniques until you get consistent and accurate results.

Divination is useful in relationships, job changes, travel, healing, and the future because it provides an unbiased view of an issue or situation. The critical factor here as with all other forms of intuition is the ability to analyze the information that is given to you without letting your emotions get too involved. Performing a meditation or grounding exercise before you begin any divination process is a good way to rid yourself of ego, reinforce your intention to use your skills for the highest good, and quiet your

The vibrational energies of crystals aid in divination practices.

mind. Remember, if you feel calm about your interpretation, it is most likely the correct analysis. Whether you like the interpretation or not is another issue.

Pendulum

Pendulums, like all other divination tools, assist you in gaining insight and information about yourself, another person, a situation, or an event. The pendulum is one of the easiest divination tools to learn and one of the simplest to use.

A pendulum is simply a string or cord to which some type of weight is tied. The weight could be a stone, key, crystal, ring, or even a paper clip or bolt. You can easily make your own by tying a favorite item onto a length of string. The pendulum moves by reacting to energy impulses from your unconscious. This impulse takes the form of the weight moving in a particular pattern in response to a "yes" or "no" question.

The pendulum is a good tool to begin divination work with as it requires little interpretation.

A pendulum will move side to side, up and down, clockwise, or counterclockwise. One of these movements will react to a "yes" response and another to a "no" response. The movement for each response is different for each person. To determine your "yes" movement, hold your pendulum in your left hand, which is your receptive hand and therefore more intuitive. Hold the cord comfortably, but lightly, between any finger and thumb. Your arm should be outstretched so that the cord and weight are hanging freely. Ask a question to which you know the answer is "yes," such as, "Is my name Joanne?" Or you can simply say, "Show me 'yes.'" The weight will begin to move in one of the four patterns mentioned above. Note this as your "yes" response. Next, ask a question to which you know the answer is "no," or say, "Show me 'no.'" Note the "no" movement of your pendulum.

One of the reasons that the pendulum is a good tool to start with is that it does not require a lot of interpretation or analysis. You will clearly get a "yes" or "no" answer. You may also get no movement at all, which means your question could be ambiguous and needs to be rephrased or the situation is too unclear to read. The skill lies in asking the right questions in the proper sequence to narrow and direct the information that is streaming from your unconscious. You may need to consider data from your analytic mind as well as past experiences when the results do not feel "right" to you. It is very important to approach the information you receive with respect and caution in order to ensure that you are interpreting the results accurately and not just "wishing" for one outcome versus another.

As you begin your intuitive journey, you'll find the pendulum a useful tool with which to explore your intuition and to prove to yourself that you really do know the answers to many questions. Over time, as your intuitive skills become more acute, you can use your pendulum to validate your analysis of your intuitive response.

It may take weeks or months of practice for your pendulum to answer consistently, but when it does you can find out answers to all sorts of things!

Practice: Fine-Tune Your Pendulum Skills

Use your pendulum in a quiet place where it is easy to concentrate. Approach the exercise with confidence that you will retrieve the correct answers to your questions and be able to interpret them accurately.

1 Clear your mind by quietly meditating for a few minutes or just focus on your breathing. You may also choose to do alternate-nostril breathing (see page 21) to bring energy to and harmonize both sides of your brain.

2 Use a deck of playing cards; shuffle them well so all the cards are in a random order.

3 Take the top card off the deck, and put it face down on a table. Hold your pendulum over the card and ask, "Is this card red?" Notice whether your pendulum moves in your "yes" pattern or "no" pattern. Turn over the card to see if you were correct. You may want to do a series of at least ten cards before turning them over to find out how well you did.

4 Keep fine-tuning your divination skills by repeating this process many times until you consistently get accurate results.

5 Next, you can try to determine the suit of the card or even the number of the card.

Remember, you already know the answer. A pendulum is just a tool to validate your intuition. Soon you will probably be able to see the card in your mind's eye (or hear it or feel it) without even using your pendulum!

The pendulum is just a tool to validate what you already know intuitively.

Uses for the Pendulum

Once you become comfortable with using your pendulum, you will be able to use your reawakened divination skill in many situations. For example:

✳ Find lost items, such as keys, jewelry, or glasses.

✳ Determine the sex of a baby before it is born.

✳ Locate the perfect place to take a vacation.

✳ Help diagnose health problems.

✳ Find a lost pet.

✳ Determine the timing of future events.

✳ Help decide which job to accept or pursue.

✳ Suggest the right time to switch jobs or ask for a raise.

✳ Help decide which baby sitter to hire.

✳ Find energy spots—areas that positively affect the body, mind, and spirit—in your house and yard.

✳ Help decide which vitamins or herbs to take.

✳ Help decide who to date.

✳ Help determine which college to attend or whether to return for an advanced degree.

✳ Suggest where to move.

✳ Help determine which service station to use and whether to trust the mechanic.

✳ Choose which books to read.

✳ Make financial decisions.

✳ Choose a gift for someone.

✳ Help decide when and where to look for a job.

The list is endless…

You can use your divination skills to answer an endless list of questions and to assist in decision making.

CHAPTER TWO *You can't be intuitive if you are trying to be right. Intuition is a silent voice or a thought that arises from your energy center. In Tai Chi, this is called your* tan-tien—*your belly center. This voice is without emotion whether or not the information it is sharing is good or bad. If fear, anger, guilt, or judgment is attached to a feeling, image, or voice, it is not your intuitive voice speaking.*

Recognize Your Unique Intuitive Skills

Intuition is an information-gathering exercise to help you collect pieces of the truth. Don't try to figure out the answer—just let the images, symbols, and voices arise, and they will lead you to the truth. Your rational brain can then apply a logical process to putting this intuitive information into a useable form. Putting the pieces together will allow you to find the meaning behind the message. If you want to make the most of your intuition, you have to slow down the tendency to rush to conclusions and analyze the message. It is often better to sit with the images and knowings for a while to see if anything else arises and notice how you feel about the message.

Notice your physical reality when you are in an intuitive state. Do you feel colder or warmer? Has your surrounding environment suddenly become quiet or do you hear everything with crystal clarity? Has your breathing changed? Is your vision sharper or fuzzier? Different sensations are clues to intuitive experiences. When you are open to receiving information, you can use your skills for a variety of purposes—telepathy, precognition, healing, remote viewing, divination.

Recognize and Follow Your Instincts

One of the first steps in developing your intuition is to recognize and learn your own symbolic language. Intuition does not speak to us in complete sentences or with complete visual clarity like a movie. It is rare to receive a literal symbol for an event that is about to occur or the underlying meaning of an issue. The stories you might have heard of a mother suddenly "seeing" her child in a swimming pool and running to the backyard to find him struggling in the water do happen, but are extraordinarily uncommon.

One reason why many of us are out of touch with our intuition is that we expect information to be handed to us in an obvious fashion. When we get just a glimpse or a simple "yes" or "no," or an image, we tend to ignore it because it does not make sense to our rational mind. But this is the way that our intuition communicates with us.

Intuition is often delivered in a jumble of symbols, sounds, and feelings that have to be interpreted and integrated by the rational, conscious mind. It is very tricky to assemble these bits and pieces in order to make sense. You need to develop a logical, problem-solving approach so that you can correctly assemble the information. The answer may be obvious, or you may have to receive more impressions to validate the answer. Dance between your intuition and rational mind to see if the rational analysis "feels right" to you. Don't be too quick to offer suggestions to someone else based on your intuitive take of a situation, or act on an issue after one divination session. It takes time to properly interpret all the information that you are receiving.

Your new skills will blossom with consistent dedication to their development. Taking the time to practice is the greatest gift you can give to your emerging intuitive self.

Be conscious of the forms of your personal symbols and how you receive that information. Although certain common images tend to mean the same things for people in the same culture (such as flying, which might signify rising above a problem), your personal interpretations are the most powerful. For example, suppose you get an image of a train when asking your intuition a particular question. A train might mean adventure, the drudgery of a commute, relocation, your life journey, or your digestive tract.

Certain archetypes (such as the Hero, the Wise Old Man, and the Great Mother) hold concentrations of psychic energy because they are so universal in their essence. When images that resonate with these archetypes appear for you, they may be sending you a deep message and should be considered with great respect and careful analysis.

You may try using your pendulum, discussed in the previous chapter, to validate what the symbol means. Ask your intuition a series of questions, such as: "Does the train indicate a relocation?" "Will the relocation occur soon?" "Within the next year?" "Within the next six months?" "Will the relocation be to the West Coast?" "To the Midwest?"

Each question should be specific and unambiguous. It should also not be a question with two parts, because you could potentially get two different answers. For instance, if you ask your intuitive self, "Will it rain tomorrow?" The answer will most likely be "yes" because it will be raining somewhere. Instead, be specific and ask, "Will it be raining when I arrive in New York City tomorrow?" A question such as, "Should I vacation in the south

The image of a train might have several different meanings, such as adventure, relocation, or your life journey.

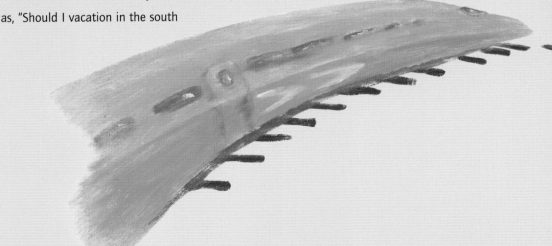

of France this year?" is also ambiguous. Be careful of the word *should,* because it implies many possibilities—such as, "You should because that is what your family expects" or "You should because it is familiar and not stressful." Rephrasing the question to, "Where is a vacation spot perfect for this August?" is more specific and will provide a clearer answer.

Use the right questions and the right sequence of questions to clarify the meaning of your symbol and provide more detailed and specific information. It is also important to know if your symbol has more relevance to the past, present, or future. This questioning technique teaches your deductive-questioning skills and intuition to work in harmony.

When you go into the unconscious to retrieve an image, the realm that you access is infinite. Images that appear are often clues to very important feelings, solutions to pressing problems, or guides on your journey to increased intuitive skills. However, sometimes the meanings of these images become clearer only later, when other images can furnish a context.

I have taken part in many guided visualizations led by prominent leaders in the sacred arts and human potential fields. While in these processes, many people ask the question, "How do I know I'm not just making up the answer or creating the vision?" Or perhaps the vision that they get seems silly or trivial or too complicated. The response from these experts is to trust your visions and answers. You might receive an answer to a question that you did not ask. Maybe you are making up the answers or the visions, but then, why did you see a waterfall and not a mouse? From personal

If a waterfall appears to you in a visualization, trust that it is an important clue on your journey.

experience, I have found that the first image I receive often evolves into something else. Also, sometimes it takes time or someone else's insight for the images to make sense.

After you ask a question, answer it by writing or talking out loud immediately. If you slow down, your rational, judgmental mind will start in and interfere with the stream of intuitive images or thoughts.

Stream-of-Consciousness Writing

One of the easiest and best skills you can use in any situation is stream-of-consciousness writing. By writing out your thoughts, no matter how unrelated, incomplete, or trivial they seem, you will begin to activate your intuition.

Without judgment or evaluation, freely let your thoughts flow. You can uncover hidden insights, or see a different angle you had not previously considered. You may also recognize a pattern that allows you to connect situations or thoughts so you can see the bigger picture or explore things more holistically.

Practice: Get Your Juices Flowing

In order to get your juices flowing, try the revealing technique of completing sentence fragments pertaining to a situation. You can make up a bunch of your own to use or get started with the following:

* I would really like it if ...
* No one understands that ...
* I would never ...
* The things I know to be true are ...
* If I could I would ...

* I don't know if ...
* It really bothers me when ...
* If I had to do it over again I would ...
* My best friend would say ...
* I don't like it when ...

Practice: Get Your Juices Flowing

Another technique is to do word associations using mind mapping. Create a mind map by writing your main thought—a situation, question, or decision—in the center of a piece of paper. As thoughts come to you, connect them with lines to your main thought. Keep related thoughts together on the same line. The mind map will resemble spokes on a wheel with words radiating out from the center. You will see a pattern emerging that will help you uncover the source of your feelings, a solution to the problem, or a new, previously unconsidered approach.

Let your thoughts flow freely to activate your intuition.

Intuitive Modes

It is necessary to be aware how your intuitive information is presented to you. Did you see a picture in your mind's eye? Did you hear sounds or voices? Or did you get a feeling or a knowing? Over time, you will develop a vocabulary of images and understand how messages are given to you.

There are three primary intuitive modes—*clairvoyance*, *clairaudience*, and *clairsentience*. Whether you see, hear, or sense the answers to your questions is highly personal.

Most people are visual. The ability to clearly see people, places, objects, scenes, or symbolic images is the most common mode and is called *clairvoyance*. The literal translation from the French is "clear seeing." This seeing is inner seeing through your mind's eye. Some visions may take on a physical form, such as an aura or a vision, but the most common are those seen during meditation or visualizations.

You can develop the skill to see images through practice; yet, for some people, this skill remains unattainable. It took me years of practice to be able to see images through visualizations, even though I paint and draw. Even now, I most often get fuzzy images that are fleeting. My intuitive knowings speak to me much more loudly through sounds and feelings. Yet my nighttime dreams are full of very detailed images in addition to sounds and feelings. Do not get discouraged if you cannot visualize. Your intuitive answers will come through to you in the manner in which you can best recognize them. I believe that the more we come to respect our intuition, the more channels open to us and the more we become aware through other senses.

One of the most famous stories showing the powers of visions is the legend of Joan of Arc. An illiterate French peasant, Joan of Arc saw visions and heard voices of angels. These voices gave her the gift of prophecy, which enabled her to initiate and carry out one of the most transformational military and political turnovers in European history.

Her visions started when she was thirteen. By the time she was seventeen, the visions of St. Catherine and St. Margaret commanded her to journey to the Dauphin's court to inspire his armies to take back the lands that led to Reims that were currently in enemy hands. The Dauphin, Charles VII, had not yet been crowned, because Reims, the place where the coronation ceremonies for French kings had been held for 1,000 years, was

Joan of Arc led France into victory by honoring the messages sent to her in the forms of visions and voices.

controlled by the English. Joan, known as the Maid of Orleans, was forbidden by her father to go on this journey, but her friends, convinced by her fervor, secured boys' clothing and a horse for her. It was inconceivable at the time that a king would allow a seventeen-year-old girl to command his armies! Yet that was precisely what The Maid convinced him to do, earning the confidence and trust of the men she led. A young girl who honored the messages sent to her in the form of visions and voices saved the kingdom of France from English domination. Yet she was burned at the stake at the age of nineteen, charged with heresy and witchcraft. The French royalty, whose country she saved, did nothing to help her.

The ability to hear sounds, voices, or music inside your head is called *clairaudience*. This term means "clear hearing" in French. Historically, this phenomenon has occurred in mystical and trance experiences as the voice of God, angels, or spirit guides communicating with saints or mystics. The ancient Greeks believed that your *daimon*, or soul-companion, whispered advice in your ears. Messages are often given this way during times of crisis as a warning in your mind. Many channelers claim to get their information from voices or messages from the dead. You, too, can communicate with loved ones if you can quiet your mind and be clear in your intention. At the beginning, try using a divination tool, such as a pendulum, to confirm your answers.

My intuition speaks to me. In asking the Universe a particular question, I will most often hear, "yes," "no," or "not yet." When the answer shifts to "yes," I will hear more detailed information. When I am creating art, particularly when I am creating a *mandala* (Sanskrit for "circle"), I hear the direction that the mandala is to take. Mandalas are used by many spiritual traditions for healing and transforming. As an artist, when I go into a meditative state to retrieve an image, the realm that I access is infinite. When any person is in a meditative state or taking part in a visualization exercise, he or she is also accessing this collective unconscious.

*Using your senses
to receive intuitive
information is
highly personal.*

Clairsentience means "clear sensing" in French and is another way of saying "empathy." Empathetic people are also called *sensitives*. They psychically receive their intuition, either internally or externally, via smell, taste, touch, emotions, and physical sensations. Some clairsentients can smell odors not present in the physical world, which can alert them to the presence of a spirit or to some event about to happen. Once you become aware of your intuitive modes, you can relate smells to a particular situation. For example, internally perceiving the smell of cigar smoke may signify to you that the person with whom you are talking is not trustworthy. Those people who are extremely clairsentient need to be aware of emotional highs and lows, particularly when those feelings have been absorbed from other people. In crowded areas or in emotional situations (such as funerals, hospitals, and even sports games), you need to protect yourself from unwanted feelings and physical sensations. Those who work in the healthcare industry need to be particularly cautious that they do not absorb the feelings of people they are treating.

I believe that we are all clairsentient to an extent, some more than others. The human body is innately intelligent and is a highly sensitive intuition receptor. We tend to live so much of our lives from the neck up, ignoring our body giving us early warning signs and clues to living more efficiently. Yet, we have all felt the hairs on the back of our neck stand up or have gotten goose bumps on our arms in particular situations. This is an example of clairsentience that may be a warning of a dangerous situation or deep knowings from a statement that was just made.

When speaking with someone else who is discussing a situation such as a job opportunity or a dream they had, I will often get a chill down my spine. This is my body's way of telling me that they will get the job, that the dream contained a powerful message for them, or that what they said was meant as a message for me. I have been in situations where my brain seems to shut off and my body takes over, particularly in situations of danger or extreme emotional discomfort where I will physically remove myself from that place without any conscious decision.

Body awareness can also be used to test for "yes" or "no" answers, much like a pendulum. The technique called muscle testing uses a body sensation—such as stickiness between the thumb and index finger, or strength or weakness in interlocking fingers to signify "yes" and "no" answers. Chapter Six discusses muscle testing in more detail.

A good friend of mine has learned to trust her body to ease her commute during New York City's rush hour. Subway cars are often jam packed. My friend's intention is always to get a seat as soon as possible. When entering a crowded car, she will let her body lead her to the most opportune place to stand in order to get the next available seat from someone who is getting off the train. Sometimes when she gets on a train, she feels as though someone is standing in her "spot" and, sure enough, the seat in front of that person is vacated at the next station stop. When she tries to think instead of let her body lead her to the best place to stand, she is always wrong. Set an intention and trust in your body's innate intelligence.

CHAPTER THREE *It is much easier to be psychic with those we love and are emotionally connected to than with a stranger or an inanimate object. Edgar Cayce has suggested that love is the key to unlocking the door to our higher consciousness. Our psychic perceptions grow stronger when we are asking for insight while holding the field of unconditional love. This is why parents and children, husbands and wives, brothers and sisters, and close friends so often report instances of telepathy or clairvoyance, especially in times of extreme need or danger. Consider relationships to be the practice grounds for developing your skills. In some situations, however, it may be easier to connect with a stranger or acquaintance because your desire for a particular outcome may cloud your interpretation of the intuitive information that you receive.*

Psychic Skills in Relationships

When we are coming from a place of fear or negativity, we block access to our psychic nature. It is important to get rid of our hostilities and resentments because they destroy the potential for intuition and keep us removed from an open and loving perspective on life. Getting rid of negativity is one of the most important things we can do to become clear channels for intuitive development.

There are many ways to get to know someone you love on a deeper level. Telepathy can help you resonate better together, psychometry can be useful for understanding a loved one's past or emotions, tarot can give you insights into a particular situation, and numerology can teach you different aspects of your loved one's personality.

Telepathy

Telepathy is one of those areas where many people have had experiences, even if they did not recognize them as psychic experiences. How many times have you finished the sentence of someone close to you or knew what they were going to say before they spoke? How often have you gotten the urge to talk with someone, only to find out that they had wanted to call you with news?

Telepathy is a skill that can be developed in a few weeks, particularly with people with whom you are close. It is the ability to communicate directly—with pictures, sounds, and words—from one person's mind to another. It is easiest to communicate this way with the people you live with, or your family, the people you work with, your friends, and the people you love.

Messages tend to pop up when your rational mind is quiet and your intuitive mind is open to receive. When you are busy juggling numerous things, your intuition does not have time to check in and see what messages might be waiting to be received. Instead, when you are relaxed, just before going to sleep or upon awakening, or while driving or engaged in physical activity is when you are most likely to hear telepathic messages.

My good friend had two psychic experiences with close loved ones who died. When she was in college, she was summoned by her mother to drive home because her father had just been taken to the hospital. She remembers being very calm, even though the friend she had been with was very concerned. On the way to the hospital, she got a sudden knowing that he had died, but a very strong, calming feeling that everything would be alright. Later, she found out that her father had died at the same moment she received the message. Many years later, she found herself suddenly and inexplicably sick, to the point that she had to lie down. These feelings started in the afternoon and were over by early evening, when she felt fine enough to go out for the night. She found out the next morning that her older brother had died midafternoon the previous day.

When I was a teenager, my grandmother had had a series of strokes and was unable to talk coherently. I often took care of her and always knew what she needed or what question she was asking. My aunt, who was her primary caregiver, could never figure out how I knew what my grandma wanted. I never understood how my aunt didn't know what my grandma needed! Although I didn't know it at the time, I was actually communicating telepathically with my grandmother. It seemed to me like the most obvious thing in the world. Most certainly, our strong family connection and my fervent desire to communicate with her opened wide our psychic channels so that we could stay in touch.

The exercises on the next page will help to build your connection with your loved ones as you become more in tune with their feelings and desires. As your intuitive channel opens up wider, you will be able to sense, even before you are face-to-face, what is going on in their lives, what they need from you, and how you can best react to them. You can validate your results easily with your loved ones, so you will learn what an intuitive experience feels like. This will give you confidence to use and expand your skills to other areas of your life.

While your rational mind is singularly focused on driving, your intuitive mind is open to receive.

Practice: Learning Telepathy

Learning telepathy is like playing a guessing game. Those games you played with friends and family members as a kid—"guess what I have in my hand" or "guess what I am thinking"—were ways to open up your psychic channels. Practicing telepathy really is a lot of fun, and you will find that you get the best results when you are at your most enthusiastic and in a good mood.

Sending Numbers

In this exercise, take turns being the sender and the receiver:

1 The sender thinks of a number from one to ten. Give it lots of energy by associating it with an object or a song. For example, you may picture the number one as a flagpole or see it as the number on your favorite player's football jersey.

2 The receiver should react with his or her first instinct, which is generally the right answer.

Thinking of Friends

Another exercise is to send messages to a friend during the day:

1 Agree to set aside the same time each day to practice communicating with each other.

2 Get rid of negative feelings, and focus on how much you love this person and how close you are to each other. Relax by doing some breathing or stretching.

3 Picture your friend in your mind's eye. What is your friend doing? How does he or she feel? What is weighing heaviest on your friend's mind? Is your friend trying to send you a particular thought? What is it?

4 Write down any impressions that you receive.

Practice telepathy by sending thoughts to a friend at a particular time of the day.

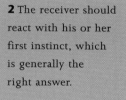

Psychometry

Psychometry is the ability to get information about the owner of an object by holding it in your hand or against the middle of your forehead, at the site of what's called the "third eye." The third eye represents mystical vision. Some animals, such as iguanas, still have a functional third eye, also called the pineal gland. There is some scientific evidence that this organ was people's first eye as well. Indeed humans still have a pineal gland, which has been linked to clairvoyance and intuition.

The term *psychometry* was first used in the mid-1800s by American physiologist Joseph R. Buchanan, who claimed it could be used to measure the "soul" of all things. Objects such as a photograph or an object that the person has owned, like a hairbrush or a glove, are used in psychometry. Buchanan believed that objects recorded senses and emotions and that these could be played back in the mind of the psychometric seer. In other words, according to psychometry, the past is contained in the present. Psychic imprints, including information about an object's owner—variously called vibrations, psychic ether, and energy—can be picked up by sensitive people.

How does psychometry work? Because our bodies give off magnetic energy fields, whenever we handle an object, we imprint information about ourselves on that object. These imprints can carry any type of information—a location, a feeling, even a favorite pastime. It is important to remember, however, that more than one person may have handled an object. Thus, its psychometric history may reveal things that are not related to a single owner. For example, if an object has been passed down through a family, it will contain information about all of its previous owners.

Strong emotions seem to be particularly evident in objects. For this reason, psychometry is particularly helpful in solving crimes, and it is the main technique used in psychic criminology. Clairvoyants are sometimes used to help in murder investigations and to locate missing persons. They will use a picture of the victim and an object that is owned by him or her to see what has happened and where it has happened. They often work with maps of the area where the victim was last seen to energetically feel where he or she traveled.

Psychometry is a good starting point when developing your psychic skills because the information received can be validated objectively. Also, because you are working with a physical object, you have something tangible on which to concentrate. A physical object helps as a bridge to connect you to your inner realms.

As you concentrate, you will see or hear parts of images, fleeting memories, or feelings. At the beginning, concentrate on being able to recognize information that can be confirmed by the person who owns the object. Knowing what it feels like to be wrong will help you understand the difference between an accurate impression and a forced one.

Objects record emotions that can be replayed in the mind of the psychometric seer.

Practice: Learning Psychometry

✳ Ask a friend to borrow an object from someone who they know but you do not. Hold the object. Relax and clear your mind. Center yourself by spending a few minutes concentrating on your breathing. Trust that you know how to read an object and that the information that will be revealed to you is accurate.

✳ As you hold the object, speak your impressions in a stream of consciousness. Let the words flow without worrying whether they sound silly, or inappropriate, or unbelievable. Speaking aloud may feel odd at first because it might be the first time you have not censored your spoken thoughts. Try to keep as open as possible by continuing to breathe and trusting in your innate abilities. The more you practice, the easier the activity will become. Ask your friend to write down your thoughts as you speak.

✳ If you have trouble getting started, ask yourself questions about the person who owns the object and let the answers arise spontaneously. The answers may be in the form of images, voices, or feelings. You will find that you have a unique style of receiving

information. No one way is right or wrong. Here are some sample questions you can use to get started:

- What adjectives describe the person—happy, worried, energetic, depressed, outgoing, shy?

- How does the person like to spend his or her time—dancing, playing baseball, race-car driving, cooking, painting, reading?

- What are the person's dreams—to get married, travel, go back to school, change professions?

- How old is the person?

- What color is the person's hair or eyes? Is he or she tall or short? Heavy or thin?

✳ Keep asking questions in your mind until you feel that you are finished. Then sit quietly to see if any other information arises.

✳ Verify your results by checking with your friend. How accurate were you? Did you come close on some points? Perhaps the person you were reading loves sports, and you said football or, perhaps the person loves to cook, and you saw a restaurant.

Remember, you are attempting to communicate in a more direct and personal way than you usually do. Normally, people put filters and biases on the information they receive. In psychometry, you are training yourself to be open to speaking thoughts that may sound foreign to you. As you move beyond your normal senses, your whole body is learning to listen. You are teaching yourself to "feel" information, as your physical mind interprets the results. The more you practice and the more deeply you believe in your innate ability to know information about other people, the more accurate you will become in your readings.

After you have practiced with a friend and are feeling more confident about your ability to ascertain true from false information, you can put your skill to practical use. Perhaps you own a cherished item from your grandmother, such as her cameo brooch or her music box. You may have been very young when she died or perhaps you did not know her at all. By holding the object and allowing thoughts to arise as you did in the above exercise, you may begin to get impressions of what her life was like—her likes and dislikes, her favorite pastimes. You can connect with her and feel a greater sense of your own history. Perhaps you will even discover that you both share a passion for chocolate-covered cherries, perhaps you will come to understand that you have always been drawn to the fuzzy leaves of violets because one of her hobbies was raising African violets. Your past is not lost to you when you can tap into the energies that your ancestors left for you to find.

Tarot Cards

Tarot is a mirror for self-reflection, a way to stop and listen to what the world has to say. A tarot deck is very practical because it is designed to give immediate input into a current situation. I have asked questions of various tarot decks over the years for clarification of a situation or when I was stuck, and the wisdom of the card has always provided insight.

The tarot can be helpful in relationship issues because the emotions involved often cloud the real issue. Use of the deck can provide a detached perspective of the situation, without the judgment of right or wrong. If you are open to perceiving the process as a gift for your individual growth and intuitive awakening, the more meaningful the messages will be for you and the more respectful you will be in dealing with the situation.

Be open to perceiving a tarot reading as a gift for intuitive awakening.

Tarot cards have been in existence for thousands of years. It is unknown whether the cards originated in China, India, or Egypt. The tarot decks that are popular today appeared in Italy and France during the fourteenth century. The deck consists of 78 cards—56 belong to the Minor Arcana, and the remaining 22 cards to the Major Arcana. The Major Arcana contains the archetypal images of the human journey, from The Fool, to The Rebel, to Change and Integration, to Completion. These cards refer to spiritual matters and important trends. The Minor Arcana refers to events or feelings that are transitory, such as playfulness, stress, sorrow, patience, and celebration.

There are many, many types of decks available today. They can be based on the original set of tarot cards, with variations in terms of the suits, the types of images associated with each card, and the meaning of each card. Also, other divination decks that do not follow the tarot—such as animal medicine cards and goddess cards—can also be used in similar ways to the tarot to gain insight about a situation. Different decks may appeal to you for meditation, for personal versus public use, or for the sheer beauty of their images. Be certain that the culture described in the cards represents your values and traditions. Also, be sure that the symbols and philosophy underlying the deck's imagery match your religious and social beliefs.

You do not have to be a trained diviner to gain valuable information from a tarot reading. Once again, intuition—which card to pick—is combined with analysis—what is this card telling me about my question or current life situation?

When a card from the Major Arcana appears in a reading, it has special significance. The current circumstances are presenting an opportunity to examine one of the central themes of your unique life journey. It can indicate that a major change is taking place. If there are no Major Arcana cards in the reading, it means that the current situation is transitory and does not represent a major issue in your life.

Tarot cards can be used as a tool to confirm what you already know.

The tarot is merely a reflection of what you already know but may be unwilling or unable to recognize at the current time. Simply by asking yourself a question in meditation or a quiet space, it is possible to access your own innate intuition for the proper response. However, it is helpful to have tools to confirm our knowings because we then gain more confidence in our own wisdom.

Practice: Using Tarot Cards

1 Quiet your mind, and enter the process with respect and with the confidence that you will receive the information you need and be able to interpret it accurately. Set up a sacred space by lighting a candle, burning some incense, or laying out a pretty cloth.

2 Do a brief meditation to ground yourself. Ask your deities or higher self that the information you receive will be for the highest good of all involved. If you are doing a reading for someone else who is present, have them join you in meditation.

Ask for guidance in interpreting the message without ego or attachment to outcome. Picture clearly the question you wish to ask.

3 When you are ready, shuffle the cards while meditating on your question. When you feel ready, fan them facedown and use your left hand— which is the receptive, intuitive hand— to select one or more cards. Alternatively, you can pull cards off the top or let them jump out of the deck, which is what I do.

4 A reading can consist of one card or a series of cards laid out in a special pattern called a spread. You can refer to the particular deck you are using to suggest various spreads in which the positions that the cards are drawn and placed have specific meanings. Ultimately, you will develop your own way of using the cards; there is no right or wrong way.

Set up a sacred space by lighting a candle, burning some incense, or laying out a pretty cloth.

Numerology

Similar to astrology in that our birth date is used to divinate meaningful information about a person's life and potential, numerology uses numbers derived from both the birth date and name as the basis for understanding an individual. Various calculations portend character traits, life purpose, motivation, and potential talents. Reading the numbers can suggest the most opportune times to make major life shifts, such as marriage, travel, or a new job. Pythagoras, the Greek mathematician, is thought to be the source of much of what we call numerology today. Pythagoras mystically associated numbers with virtues, colors, and many other ideas. He spoke of how our life paths reflect eternal laws, and he pointed to numerical patterns that served as keys for unlocking secrets of the psyche.

The Life Path is the most important number in numerology. It represents who you are at birth and the inherent traits that will be a part of you throughout life. My Life Path number is 1. My drive is characterized by independence and creative inspiration. The negative traits associated with this path are overconfidence and impatience. The Expression number is derived from all the letters of your full name. This number describes your life's purpose with all the talents that are at your disposal. My Expression number is 9, which is characteristic of humanistic interests as well as strong creative ability. The negative traits associated with this number are self-centeredness and aloofness.

Other cultures, such as some indigenous tribes in Africa, also combine the birth year with a numerical representation of the letters of your full name to determine your characteristics and tendencies. For example, in the Dagara tribe, I would be considered an Earth person, yet I have an overabundance of Fire. Earth people are nurturing and empowering. However, an abundance of Fire suggests that I can exhibit aggression and impatience.

Why is it important to understand our own and other's characteristics? When we are able to understand a loved one from a more objective viewpoint, we can become more compassionate and forgiving about certain behaviors. Saying, "Why can't you be more outgoing, detail-oriented, independent, emotional, or tolerant?" is not helpful if that person's basic personality traits do not lend themselves easily to those attributes. Instead, when we are aware of a person's positive traits, we can help that person aspire to their full life potential.

Your Life Path number represents your inherent traits.

Practice: Find Your Life Path Number

• To determine your Life Path number, write your birth date numerically—for example,

5-17-1963

• Put a plus sign between each digit and add them all up—for example,

5+1+7+1+9+6+3=32

• Add the digits of the sum together—for example,

3+2=5

If your sum ends in a zero, such as 10, 20, or 30, you need to again add the two digits of the sum together—for example,

1+0 = 1

This is your Life Path number.

Calculating the Life Path numbers of your friends and family will reveal meaningful information about their characteristics and potential.

Life Path Number Descriptions in Brief

1: This path is characterized by independence and creative inspiration. The negative traits associated with this path are overconfidence and impatience.

2: These are extremely sensitive people who have a sincere concern for others. Their biggest obstacle is overcoming passivity and a state of apathy and lethargy.

3: This path emphasizes expression and excellence in social situations; however, there is a tendency for these people's lives to become frivolous and superficial.

4: These people are trustworthy, practical, and down-to-earth; however, they can also become narrow-minded, and repressive.

5: This path emphasizes being adventurous and always striving to find answers. The negative aspects of this path are self-indulgence and irresponsibility.

6: These people have a strong sense of responsibility and are idealistic. However, they can also be overwhelmed by responsibilities and overly critical of themselves or others.

7: This path is characterized by peaceful and affectionate souls, who are naturally reserved and analytic. However, they can become very pessimistic, quarrelsome, and secretive.

8: The positive qualities of this path produce many powerful, confident, and materially successful people. However, this independent and competitive nature exhibits itself negatively in dictatorial actions that suppress the enthusiasm and efforts of others.

9: These people are compassionate, generous, tolerant, and broad-minded. Their main negative trait is that they have difficulty believing in the humanitarian value of their path.

CHAPTER FOUR *Intuition is the best kept secret of business decision-making. There are numerous instances of chief executives and successful business people acting on hunches that seemed financially unstable or unworkable at the onset but proved to be wise decisions in retrospect. I usually had a "gut feeling" about the success or timing of a project that invariably proved to be true. However, it's hard for managers to heed those nagging voices from somewhere deep inside without sounding unprofessional or questioning their sanity. It is suspect in the business world to talk openly about how you "feel" about a situation, or your "gut reaction."*

Psychic Skills at Work

Although many managers may find basing decisions on intuition to be too subjective and not sufficiently analytic, it is slowly becoming a valid subject in corporate thinking and training. Incorporating and encouraging practices that are open to the intuitive process can help companies avoid myopic reliance on the numbers, which narrows the corporate vision and limits its long-term success. Instead, a culture of innovation and calculated risk taking sets the stage for identifying and responding to industry opportunities.

The business world has traditionally been dominated by left-brain thinking. This hemisphere handles the logical and linear functions, whereas the right hemisphere provides the creative impulse. In combination, intuition enhances analytic thinking by providing insights to timing, specific strategy, and innovation. Once one realizes that the intuitive process can provide an industry advantage as well as a personal edge in the office, using psychic skills at work becomes a critical factor to success and survival in the corporate world.

The "Aha!" Moment

Becoming intuitive is the process of opening up to one's creativity. Researchers have mapped this process into four stages—preparation, incubation, illumination, and verification. In the preparation stage, one acquires a skill set, gathers some data, or understands the basic problem that needs to be addressed. This is where the left brain—the analytic functions—come into play. Picture the tennis player hitting a serve over and over again, or the business executive reading the daily paper looking for trends.

In the incubation stage, the unconscious takes over to solve the problem. The conscious mind is not actively working to seek a solution. An "aha!" moment requires the alternation of intense conscious work and relaxation. This is why it is so important for managers to be able to shut out the world for some amount of time every day to contemplate issues and to give space for illumination to occur. In this illumination moment, the unconscious processing becomes conscious and can be verbalized. It is a firm knowing or conviction that one is correct regardless of the facts and figures or how things were done before.

Here is a simple example. I have discovered when I am trying to solve a problem, if I get up and do something else, such as washing my hands, making a cup of tea, or taking a walk around the block, that suddenly the solution or an insight will come to me in a flash and will seem very obvious. I know that when I am stuck, no amount of sitting and staring at my computer screen or paperwork will conjure up the solution. I need to change my physical situation and do something else, and then the illumination has space to occur.

In the final stage, the idea is verified. Although, in some instances, the outcome cannot be proven immediately, eventually others will see that the new approach or idea had the intended outcome and was the right direction to take.

In the often frenetic business world, it is difficult to give an idea or insight the time it needs to incubate and develop into a workable business opportunity. However, if intuition is to work, some quiet contemplative time must be set aside. This creative thinking time allows for the "aha!" moment.

Getting to illumination—the "aha!" moment— may require a change of scenery.

Success Stories

It is easy to understand intuition in action by observing athletes. The most accomplished athletes claim that their peak performances never occur when they are thinking about how to do something. At these times they are playing with unthinking spontaneity. Athletes do not have time to think when a ball is hurtling at them at 90 miles per hour. Years of training are compressed into seconds of decision making. When they hit that ball, they are in a flow state— one of increased clarity and the feeling of being in total control. Athletes just know when they are going to complete a pass, hit a serve, or win a particular game. This knowing is based on confidence—and hours or years of preparation. It is similar to a business situation in which one gets a feeling to invest in a certain technology, to expand or retract a portion of the company, or to allot a certain amount of time for a new system implementation. But these feelings happen only after one has extensive knowledge in the field and has done everything to prepare for the event and pave the way.

The founders of Mrs. Fields Cookies, Federal Express, and Mary Kay Cosmetics all started their businesses intuitively. In retrospect, it may seem that they had a stroke of good fortune. However, their success was predicated by a deep knowledge of their field and a conviction that their product was needed in the marketplace and would be a grand success. All of them used business techniques that were considered unusual or controversial for the time, but that have since become standard practice.

For instance, in 1977, Debbi Fields gave out free samples of her cookies on the street to attract customers. Today, one would think nothing of seeing free samples of a product in a store or of using a software product for a free trial period. Yet she literally gave her product away, which rationally is not the way to run a business. Her intuition was verified as revenues have steadily increased to close to $175 million in 2002.

The founder of Federal Express reinvented the way that packages were delivered. When Frederick W. Smith was a student at Yale University, he came up with an idea for a term paper that tossed aside the traditional means of delivery as defined by the U.S. Postal Service. As he flew combat missions in Vietnam, he continued to work on his idea by constantly refining various aspects. His highly profitable idea has spawned a bunch of imitators, the U.S. Postal Service included, yet he barely got a passing grade on his college paper!

Intuition is more reliable than data. In a world of increasing change, complexity, and too much information, the skill to see beyond the individual factors, components and analytics is a skill worth developing.

Years of training are compressed into seconds of decision making.

9-to-5 Intuition in Practice

Do first impressions really count? Recruitment is one area where intuition can prove particularly relevant. There are stories in which managers have not hired someone on a hunch—though the applicant fit the job qualifications perfectly—only to find out later that the candidate was a convicted felon or lied on his or her résumé. Managers are better off listening to their first impressions and asking themselves why they feel as they do. Getting others involved in the interviewing process, even for a brief five-minute "hello," can help to confirm those initial impressions and lead to wiser hiring decisions. During many years of interviewing candidates, my impression, gathered in the first few minutes of meeting a person, was typically validated during the interview. If I was uncertain about a candidate, I would have a trusted colleague speak with the person for a few minutes to get an impression. By having another person validate my uncertainty, it was easier to reject an otherwise qualified candidate based on a "feeling."

First impressions should also be given attention when you are looking for a new job or to switch departments in your current company. Ask yourself, "How do I really feel about this job?" You may find that a job that looks great on paper may feel "uncomfortable," or that jobs that look merely mediocre on paper feel "right" when you walk through the door of the hiring company. Here are a few things to consider before making any decision:

"First impressions" are really your intuitive insight screaming to be heard.

❋ Stop and ask yourself how you really feel about what you are about to do.

❋ Pay attention to the first answer that surfaces, and try to avoid judging it.

❋ Involve your coworkers or staff in decisions by asking them if they have reservations, even if they cannot be quantified, about the decision.

❋ Be attentive. Catching that first impression, which is your intuitive insight screaming to be heard, takes practice. If you are unsure what you are feeling, ask yourself, "If I had to make a decision right now, what would it be?"

Keep track of your impressions and results. Once you see how accurate your intuition is, you will gain confidence in your skill and pay more attention to your hunches and gut instincts.

On the job, a leader needs to be able to feel the pulse of the office or the industry. Walking around the office, shop floor, or marketplace and gauging the mood is an important part of the preparation process for setting off that intuitive spark. I practiced this technique, coined Management by Walking Around, and found it to be invaluable in heightening my intuition. You see things that you wouldn't see if you were closeted in your office. By watching, you may become aware of what you don't know, which often stimulates intuition. The pondering or daydreaming that occurs while you are walking around gives you the time to look at old mistakes and analyze the chances of future success. Also, you can reap the benefits of other's intuition by observing and listening to different ways of seeing things, as each employee will have a unique perspective.

Intuitive workers are particularly helpful when exploring new business opportunities, attempting to cut costs, or looking into unique solutions for a problem. Slow, rational, and analytical reasoning does not work in an environment with no predetermined rules and procedures, because there is little existing knowledge to fall back on. People who can make rapid, emotionally based intuitive decisions are invaluable because they can come up with multiple ideas and options. Because intuitive employees set no standards or limits on processing their thoughts, they will eventually come up with a unique and workable idea. This idea can be supported by data if necessary. However, trying a new idea by turning it into an action speeds up decision making and results in an outcome that is potentially faster than the time it would take to "run the numbers." If this solution fails, little time has been lost and another solution can be tested. Trying to come up with options through a logical sequence of analyzing ideas may not provide the best results in a new venture.

Practice encouraging intuition in your coworkers and staff. Anyone in the organization may have a hunch about where the company needs to go or how to handle a specific situation. Gathering intuitive insights, perhaps by walking around, can greatly increase the chances for business success. Encourage employees to follow up on hunches and communicate this information. An intuitive suggestion may not conform to rules and regulations. It may be an idea before its time. Weeks or months of incubation time may be needed for an idea to coalesce, allowing key industry factors to emerge before the plan is ready to come together.

Intuition can play an important part in both planning and implementing a collective vision. In today's rapidly changing world, it is virtually impossible to prove with numbers that a particular vision is the right one. Without a leap of faith, guided by intuition, you risk limiting your personal business potential.

The following sections give you a few suggestions for accessing and verifying your intuition. Some of the other practices in this book can also be used at work. However, using a pendulum or tarot cards in your office may be just a bit extreme for even the most progressive company! The best thing about being intuitive is that it needs no fancy equipment, special lighting, or secret handshake. No one even needs to know that you are doing it. They will just wonder why you are right all the time!

Positive Imagery

What do successful business people and athletes have in common? Confidence in the ability to imagine a positive outcome. Imagery is a flow of thoughts that one can see, hear, feel, smell, or taste in one's imagination. When a tennis player is going up for a serve, all the senses are alive as he or she can see, feel, hear, smell, and taste the successful outcome even before the racket makes contact with the ball. This image of a successful serve represents internal reality. These internal images are so vivid that they manifest as external reality. Many native tribes believe that the world is as you dream it. Therefore, if you can see all the details of a positive outcome and focus your energies on their fruition, like a successful serve, you will create a successful business project.

If you doubt your ability to create something physical or material from imagination, think of the effects of worry or fear. Worry results in butterflies in the stomach, a tightening in the shoulders, a headache, or even ulcers. The body is not reacting to external events, but to thoughts or images about these events. Similarly, confidence and optimism about a particular endeavor will result in a proud stance and bright eyes, and will inspire others to join in the task.

Take that leap of faith to increase your business potential.

Positive imagery interrupts negative images and thoughts that stress you and allows the greatness of your potential to shine through and manifest itself.

Practice: Mini-vacation in Your Mind

When you need to get away or to provide quiet time for idea incubation, take a mini-vacation in your mind. Imagine you are on vacation in your favorite spot, or just imagine a peaceful place that you enjoy. If you are in the woods, imagine feeling the dappled sun on your face as it peeks through the treetops. Hear the breeze rustling the leaves and the birds chirping. Smell the pine trees and the fresh air. Feel the bark of the tree on your back as you lean against it. Try to experience this place with all your senses. Five minutes is all you need to feel refreshed. If you are trying to figure out the solution to a problem, you may find that the answer arises while you are on this mini-vacation.

The world is as you dream it—focus your energies on a positive outcome.

Channeling

Channeling is often described as the process of receiving words and information from an entity that is no longer living but that is aware of what's happening on the physical and the spiritual planes. The early demonstrations of mediumship involved table lifting, rapping, creaking of chandeliers, and other physical affects to prove that contact with the spirits had been made. Although logical explanations could not be found for some of the events during these séances, today most mediums communicate messages verbally.

If we can accept that dying is not the end of our existence, just the end of our physical body, then does our spirit or consciousness survive and exist in some other dimension? If this is so, it might be possible to make contact with that consciousness and tap into the knowledge, emotions, and memories that made that person who he or she was. Many people believe that spirits exist all around us, but are at a different frequency or vibration than those who are living. By learning to adjust to this frequency, much like tuning into a radio station, a medium can access those spirits who wish to communicate.

There are different ways that mediums communicate with spirits. Mediums can be clairvoyant in that they actually see images, scenes, or people. They might be clairaudient in that they hear voices, sometimes with accents and speech patterns that help in identifying the spirit. If a medium is clairsentient, he or she may get a physical sensation of a headache or feel fear or a general sense of well-being from the spirit, particularly as a way to communicate how he or she died. Spirits can also send scents to mediums to help in their recognition. This may be exhibited by a certain perfume, pipe tobacco, or smell associated with their occupation. A medium does not have to be in a trance to receive any of the above information. In a trance, the spirit takes over the medium's body to deliver a message to the persons present with the medium.

Why would anyone want to channel a spirit? They may want to contact a family member or someone who was close to them to see if he or she is happy, to ask an unresolved question about death perhaps, to ask for guidance in a particular situation, or to ask for his or her expertise.

Find the approach to capturing information that works best for you (see Practice on page 73). You may want to write down any impressions that came to you while you were recalling your mother. Also, you may want to review your automatic writing to see what gems can be gleaned from the words. Perhaps you received a lot of images of shoes. Your mother may be trying to tell you to "step into your coworker's shoes." By seeing the situation from his or her vantage point instead of your own, perhaps you will discover that some of your actions could have been misconstrued. Unknowingly, your own actions might have contributed to a break down in relations. You could also get to know your coworker better. You may find out that he or she is a caregiver for an elderly parent and is having trouble balancing his or her home and work life. A bit more compassion on your part may go a long way to smoothing your relationship issues. Take the time to listen and reflect on the information given to you.

Find a quiet space to communicate with the spirit world and believe in your ability to connect with its essence.

Perhaps you are trying to learn a new language that will help you to better communicate with your coworkers who are from a different country. Or perhaps you want to come up with an outstanding design for a building contest, or design an advertising campaign for a new product. Think about experts or people you admire who are leaders in that particular field. For an innovative new design, Leonardo da Vinci would be a perfect mentor! You can use the same techniques described earlier to either meditate on that person's essence or use automatic writing to get ideas about how they would

Practice: Learning Channeling

Although it may seem quite farfetched to use channeling at work, if we take the essence of channeling and apply it to solving a business problem, it can be quite useful. For example, perhaps you are having problems getting along with one of your coworkers. You remember that your mother was always able to see the best in others and was skilled in negotiating to get what she wanted, with all sides feeling like they had won.

That evening, when you get home or in the confines of a quiet office, take deep breaths and quiet your mind. Recall images and actions of your mother in various situations where she exhibited these qualities. Try to get in touch with her emotional state during these times.

Ask her how she would handle your situation, and wait for a response. Let her knowledge flow into you via words, voices, senses, or pictures.

You can also try to contact a spirit through automatic writing. This is the process of letting your own hand write without being conscious of what words or thoughts you are putting to paper. Often, writing with your nondominant hand will help to get rid of judgments coming from your conscious mind. This process can also be referred to as stream-of-consciousness writing because there is no filtering process involved in deciding what to write. Let the information flow. Do not stop to think about what you are writing.

proceed in your situation. Consider the information you receive a divine download! Similar to how you download new software onto your computer, you can also download new information into your psyche. Consciously ask to be connected to the architectural essence of Leonardo Da Vinci and expect to be connected. Belief in your ability to tap into his design knowledge is paramount in order to have a successful download of information. Ask yourself, "What kind of building would Leonardo design?" By envisioning what he would do in your particular situation, you are opening up your channels to thinking like him and tapping into the universal architect. Let the images and words flow, and capture them so that you can consciously analyze them later.

CHAPTER FIVE *Each one of us has a healing instinct, although it may have become buried under mounds of information from advertisers, the medical profession, and well-meaning friends. Food cravings are a simple example of this instinct; we might crave bananas because our bodies need potassium, or we might crave a hamburger because we need protein. Dreams are often a potent source of healing advice (see Chapter Seven), although their messages might be cloaked in symbols.*

Health and Healing

Your mind has a tremendous capacity to heal your body. You can focus your intuition to improve and potentially cure any health situation. Nobody likes pain, but by recognizing pain or disease, you give your intuitive mind permission to communicate with that pain and find out what it is trying to tell you. Remember that pain in your neck? Well, it won't go away; it will most likely get worse or show up somewhere else unless you ask questions and learn why your pain exists and what you can do to encourage healing.

Sometimes it takes the voice of a trusted expert such as a doctor or shaman to awaken your healing instinct and give it permission to go to work. The trick is in getting past your resistance. People react better when they have a strong belief in either the doctor or the treatment. Shamans say that they don't heal you, they just open up the possibilities for you to heal yourself. Many of the rituals surrounding the shamanic healing experience and the tasks to be carried out after the healing session, such as burning a green candle for five days, are intended not only to keep high energy around the experience but also to remind you that you also play a major role in your healing. Positive beliefs, emotions, and actions are essential factors for good health.

Auras

When we say that someone has animal magnetism, are we really just reacting to his or her aura? An aura is vibrational energy that radiates around everyone and everything. The combination of molecules that makes us feel solid are actually particles that are vibrating. Auras exist around living things, such as people, animals, and plants, as well as objects, such as stones, crystals, and water. The color and form around living things changes with time or as human emotions or thoughts change. The aura around objects is essentially permanent.

Auras, vibrational energies that exist around everything, can be seen by children naturally.

Each aura has a unique color and form. Auras are found in the colors of the rainbow, from purple, blue, green, yellow, orange, and red, to gray and black. A particular color is generally thought to reveal certain aspects of a person, but your intuitive nature should also be used to differentiate the meaning within the shades of colors.

Children see auras naturally, but by the time they are in school they usually lose the capability to see them because others tell them there is no such thing. Adults have a hard time overcoming this early implanted belief and may have a difficult time relearning to see auras. I have a friend whose mother started seeing auras spontaneously when she reached midlife. This occurred in a restaurant and she had no idea why everyone in the restaurant and their jewelry were glowing different colors. She has since learned to harness her powers so that she can choose when to see auras and energy levels of the people and objects around her.

Your aura embodies your true self. It is thought that disease actually starts in the energy bodies/auras around physical bodies, and is caused by physical or emotional imbalance, negative thought forms, or emotional patterns. Therefore, it is possible to see signs of disease in yourself and

Aura Colors and Human Qualities

This is a general overview of the aura colors and the human qualities associated with them:

* Purple—intuitive, spiritual

* Blue—calm, balanced, truthful

* Green—charming, healer, good listener

* Yellow—intellectual, well-being, deep inner wisdom

* Orange—friendly, inspiring, thoughtful, optimistic

* Red—physical energy, stamina, sexuality

* Gray/Black—illness, shielding

Practice: Find Your Aura

First, you need to know how large your aura is and what shape it is. You can have a friend help you by rubbing his or her hands together until they are tingling and then, starting at about two feet away, bringing them closer to your body until they feel some resistance. This is the edge of your aura. To know what this resistance feels like, rub your hands together as before and slowly bring them together, in front of you, palms facing each other, until you can feel the edges of your own energy reflecting off your palms. Once you are aware of the boundaries of your own aura, it becomes easier to consciously visualize your aura contracting around you as if it were a shield. You can do this if you are in an intense situation and do not want to absorb any negative energy. Play with your own edges to feel the difference.

others before anything manifests physically. You can heal yourself by consciously controlling your aura, and because the energy flows both ways. Your physical body affects your energy body, and your energy body also affects your physical body.

People with very open auras can unintentionally let negative energy, such as fear, shame, anger, or depression, from other people enter into their energy fields, potentially contributing to disease. Therefore it is important to be able to shield yourself so that energy that is not for your highest good will be reflected off of your aura and not be allowed to penetrate your energy space.

You can also protect yourself by reinforcing the outer edges of your aura with colored light. Surrounding yourself in white light will only allow those energies of a similar or higher vibration to enter into your space. When I am driving, I surround myself and my car in white light. I can feel the layer of protection around me, and I can expand it if I feel a car is coming too close to me. More often than not, the person in the other car will react to the expansion of white light and back off. You might also try surrounding yourself in blue light or purple light to repel negative energy. Practice with different colors, and see which ones work for you. Being responsible for your own energy body is a good first step toward awareness of the health of both your energy and your physical body, and confidence in your ability to correct disease and maintain a high level of positive spiritual energy.

Rubbing your hands together allows you to feel your own vibrational energy.

Practice: How to See Auras

You should be relaxed and comfortable in your surroundings. It will be easier to see the aura if the room is dimly lit.

✳ Have your friend sit or stand in front of a plain background, such as a soft white wall or light background.

✳ Focus on the middle of your friend's forehead—the third eye.

✳ After about 30 to 60 seconds, soften your gaze to see with your peripheral vision. Remember to keep your focus on the spot in the center of your friend's forehead.

✳ As you remain focused, you should see a white glow behind the person about an inch or two from his or her body. This is the aura.

✳ Gradually, you will see one or several colors a few inches around the body. The colors may fluctuate.

✳ You can also see your aura by sitting or standing about 4 feet away from a large mirror and following the same instructions.

Intuitive Healing

Because our bodies are energy, when there are blockages or imbalances they can manifest as many different symptoms. Because our attitudes are also an energy form, we can physically impact our bodies. A positive attitude helps to create optimal wellness. A negative attitude obstructs our path to wellness. Arthritis, physical pain, depression, digestive disorders, and fatigue may be related to deep-seated fears, old belief systems, or actual life events. These issues create congestion and stop the flow of energy to certain parts of our bodies. Intuitive healing can help us to recognize and then shift these energy blockages, thereby allowing energy to move into the congested areas and promote healing.

To strive for optimal health, you must be able to decipher the way your body communicates current and old emotions that are experienced as sensations, pain, and disease. To do this, you must be willing to honor your body's wisdom and not react with your analytical mind. Physical exercise of any kind is an important way to truly be in your body and be aware of how your body moves—its strengths and weaknesses—and how it feels on different days. Once you are more aware of your body, you will be able to pick up early warning signs that your body sends to you. The way your body speaks with you is unique, and yet there are universal symbols relating organs and certain areas of the body to particular emotions.

Chinese medicine believes that problems in the body's organs are related to emotional behavior or situations that are similar to the organ's functions. The heart is associated with joy and contentment; the liver and gallbladder are associated with the emotions of frustration and anger. For example, people who drink to excess are often angry and have an explosive temper—their livers are overwhelmed trying to get rid of too many toxins from excessive amounts of alcohol. The lungs and large intestine are related to worry and grief. For instance, a disease in the bowel, which releases waste, has to do with letting go of things or beliefs that are no longer necessary. The spleen and stomach have to do with overthinking or too much worrying.

The energy in the body that affects all the organs is called *chi* (pronounced "chee") in Chinese medicine. (This concept will be explained more fully in the next section.) It is important to be able to sense this energy and recognize when it is blocked or sluggish so that we can correct it. When we are in touch with our bodies, feeling its life force—its chi—can be a sensual experience. Just the act of tapping into this energy is a healing action.

It is very frightening sometimes to listen to our bodies and the voice of our own intuition, because then we have to acknowledge issues in our life and confront and resolve them. It seems easier to take medication to mask the emotions in our body and numb our pain. Yet pain and health are important indications of what is good and what we need to continue (how wonderful we feel after a yoga class or a dinner prepared with fresh organic ingredients!) and what is bad and needs to be adjusted (watching too much television and consuming too many sodas and snacks!).

It is also often easier to listen to your analytic side when it comes to dealing with your health, because the medical profession in the West is so predominant. Your intuition can easily be drowned out from all the advertisements and information about medication

Yoga is a good way to get in touch with your body's own life force.

formulated to solve all our problems. Trusting your inner wisdom by spending time connecting with your intuition in all the ways discussed throughout this book will help you to sort through all these external messages and find the right combination of approaches to optimally benefit you.

Your dreams are also a wonderful source of healing information. Be aware of symbols that may signal an impending health problem, or information about a current course of medication that you are taking in order to remedy an illness. Get a second opinion about a health concern by consulting your intuition via dream incubation. (Follow the suggestions for incubating your dreams in Chapter Seven.) Be sure to be specific—you may need to break up the question into a series of dream nights. What is the underlying issue? What course of action should I follow? Should I wait or proceed now? Should I switch doctors? You can also use divination tools to help to clarify your intuitive instincts.

In suggesting that illness is related to memories in the body and the different ways of dealing with emotions, you need to be careful not to feel like a victim and also not to feel like you are being blamed for your disease. It is a question of being aware of how actions and emotions in your lifetime are correlated to certain diseases and of realizing that there is a multipronged approach to returning to health. For example, undergoing heart bypass surgery and then continuing to ignore unresolved anger is not a holistic approach to health care.

You are being intuitive about your body's health when you can tap into your own emotional patterns and the images, voices, and feelings that your body is sending to you. This intuition information can help you figure out the physical, genetic, environmental, and nutritional impacts on the emotional aspects of your health.

All of us, I believe, have as a goal the feeling of being completely whole and healthy. When we feel joy, passion, and love, we feel it in every cell in our body. It is not localized to certain areas like negative emotions. When we feel this, we know we are on the right path and we feel well in a true holistic sense.

Practice: Sending Healing Energy...

...To Your Body

1 Rub your hands briskly together until you feel them tingling. Imagine the part of your body that needs healing, and send the energy through your hands from the Universe to that area. You might feel warmth in that particular part of your body.

2 Imagine the energy opening up the blockages to release fresh energy to shift old fears and belief systems. You don't have to know what the fears or beliefs are—just that they are no longer necessary and no longer serving you.

...To Your Plants

1 To see the power of healing energy you can also practice with your plants. Select a few to send healing energy to. Do they look different from your other plants?

We can send healing energy to our plants as well as to ourselves and all other living beings.

Chi Energy

Chi must be able to move freely throughout the body for good health. Practices such as Tai Chi help to open up the channels of energy in our bodies, remove blockages, and direct the energy throughout the body to attain optimal health and create a balance between body, mind, and spirit.

Tai Chi is centuries old and has enjoyed increasing popularity in this country in recent years because of the positive effects on health and the mind. The practice was derived from the martial arts and consists of slow, conscious movements and deep breathing. Tai Chi harmonizes the opposite forces in the universe, which Tai Chi practitioners and the Chinese call *yin* and *yang*. Tai Chi brings you into greater harmony with the natural world, with many of its movements imitating those of animals and birds.

According to legend, the movements of Tai Chi were inspired by a dream involving a snake and a crane.

Legend says that the movements for Tai Chi came to a martial artist in a dream. His dream was about a snake and a crane engaged in battle. Their graceful motions inspired this noncombative style of martial arts—a powerful example of listening to one's dreams!

Tai Chi consists of movement, meditation, and deep breathing. All the major muscle groups and joints are used in its deliberate and easy movements. This improves functions such as balance, strength, flexibility, and coordination. The meditation aspect soothes the mind while lowering blood pressure and heart rate. Stale air and toxins are eliminated from the body via deep breathing, while the entire body is supplied with fresh oxygen and nutrients.

While engaged in completing a Tai Chi form, which is a series of 20 to 100 different movements, your focus would remain on your *tan-tien*, the area just below your belly that the Chinese believe to be the place from which chi flows. A form can take up to 20 minutes to complete and has names that describe its movement such as "wave hands like clouds," "brush dust against the wind," and "push the boat with the current."

Apart from the energy effects on the body and mind, Tai Chi is beneficial for heart disease, high blood pressure, arthritis, headaches, depression, asthma, digestion, and gastrointestinal conditions.

A good friend of mine, who recently turned 80 years old, has been practicing Tai Chi for more than 40 years. She is more limber than many people half her age, she is in excellent health and, most importantly, she is a highly creative, involved, "full of life" being. I know that Tai Chi is an important part of her health rituals—for mind, body, and spirit. She is truly an inspiration for the benefits of living a long life rich with meaning and a connection to a higher source.

This practice is helpful in making you more aware of your body, more conscious of the connection between mind, body, and spirit, and better able to recognize the energy patterns in your body. Being aware of your energy will assist you in various forms of intuitive healing. Finding and staying with an energy practice, such as Tai Chi, that appeals to you will help you in your quest for optimal health.

The best way to learn Tai Chi is to find an experienced instructor in your area who can guide you through the movements and help you to correct your form.

Being aware of your energy will assist you in various forms of intuitive healing.

Practice: Learning Tai Chi

The basic pose in Tai Chi is called the Unpolarized Pose. Essentially, it is a relaxed standing posture that balances the nervous system and internal organs and prepares the mind for other poses. This is also a good way to center yourself before doing any divination or intuitive work.

The Unpolarized Pose

✵ Stand straight with your feet parallel, shoulder-width apart. Relax with your head high and shoulders dropped. Your arms should hang softly with your palms facing the thighs. Draw in your chin, chest, belly, and buttocks to keep your spine straight. Close your eyes slightly.

✵ Focus attention on your tan-tien.

✵ Breathe deeply through your nose. Contract your lower abdomen while breathing in, and push it out while breathing out.

Pressing the Chi Down Pose

The purpose of this pose is to get you to recognize the feeling of chi in your own body.

✵ Start in the Unpolorized Pose as described to the left.

✵ Raise your arms forward to chest height, with elbows soft, palms facing down. As you continue to raise your hands a little higher than the head, gradually turn your palms to face each other. Imagine that you are holding a big ball. Begin to lower your arms as you turn your palms downward. Finish with your hands at your stomach, near your tan-tien.

✵ Breathe in while raising your arms, and breathe out while lowering them. Feel the chi filling your tan-tien when your hands are in front of your body.

CHAPTER SIX *Every day when we step out of our homes to go to work, to school, to run errands, or to meet a friend, we make decisions about how to get there. Should we walk, bike, or drive? Which road shall we take? Most often, we follow the same path out of habit or convenience, yet sometimes we hear a voice telling us to take a different way or leave at a different time, and we avoid an accident or come upon someone who needs help.*

Psychic Skills on the Road

Vacation traveling is one area where we tend to let our defenses down because we are in holiday mode. I have done a lot of traveling throughout Asia and Europe as a single woman traveling alone. I rely heavily on my intuition to avoid dangerous situations, intuitively walk to wonderful places to eat and unusual sites, and know where to visit next.

A few skills that are handy when traveling are the awareness of remote objects, persons, or events, which is called *remote viewing*; the ability to check with your body's innate intelligence to determine the right food, place to stay, or person to trust; the ability to remove obstacles from your path, which is known as *psychokinesis*; the ability to sense energy centers in an area and to ground yourself when necessary.

Muscle Testing

Muscle testing is a useful skill while traveling to keep healthy, in deciding where to eat, what to eat, whom to trust, and where to spend the night. Decisions such as these are important, especially when visiting a foreign country.

As with the pendulum, muscle testing involves asking specific, nonambiguous questions to get accurate responses. Your body acts as the pendulum using its innate intelligence, which knows what is good for it and what isn't. Many nutritionists use this method when testing for necessary vitamins, minerals, and herbs. Chiropractors use it to find which parts of the body need adjustment and to check if an adjustment has been successfully made.

Muscle testing is based on internal energy flows that signify what effect situations or things will have on us.

Muscle testing is based on internal energy flows; when you ask a question or hold something that is not good for you, your muscles will become weaker to signify a negative impact on the body's energy flows. The body is aligned with your intuitive mind rather than your analytic mind. It can give accurate answers unknown to your conscious without being biased or suffering from wish fulfillment. Asking a question that has a positive answer or holding a bottle of vitamins that is needed by your body will result in stronger muscles signifying a positive impact.

Innate intelligence is the knowledge that every living being is born with, which allows it to survive. Plants will turn their leaves to the sun, and roots will travel in search of water. Our innate intelligence keeps our hearts beating, nutrients flowing, and infection-fighting cells traveling to areas where they are needed without conscious effort on our part.

Therefore our bodies know exactly what they need and how to adapt to the surrounding environment to perform at a high level and will always attempt to function at that level. For example, my husband doesn't like apples. Our chiropractor tested him for allergies and foods that did not serve his body well, and apples were on the list!

Train your mind for a few minutes every day, and in a few weeks you will be able to notice the difference in your muscle resistance to any question that you pose.

Practice: Learning Muscle Testing

With practice, you can train yourself to respond to a "yes" or "no" question, like you did with the pendulum exercise.

❋ Begin with a meditation or grounding exercise in which your intention is for the highest good. Ask for guidance from your higher self in interpreting and using the received information properly.

❋ Touch each thumb to the middle finger of each hand and interlock them to form two linked rings.

❋ Train yourself for a yes response by silently or out loud saying something true like "My name is Joanne" or "This is a 'yes,'" while pulling your linked fingers against each other, but don't allow them to separate. This trains your muscles to remain strong and resistant when you try to unlock your fingers in response to questions with a "yes" response.

❋ Train yourself for a no response by saying something false such as "My name is Paul" or "This is a 'no,'" while pulling your linked fingers against each other, deliberately separating them as though they were repelling each other. This trains your muscles to go weak and provide little resistance when you are trying to unlock your fingers in response to questions with a "no" response.

❋ Another way to train yourself is by putting something you are allergic to or that is unhealthy, such as a cigarette or saccharin, under your arm or in your pocket and testing for a "no" result. Then hold a bottle of vitamins or a vegetable and test for a "yes" response.

Psychokinesis

We all have the potential to be psychokinetic. The term psychokinesis *comes from the Greek words* psyche, *meaning "breath" or "life," and* kinein, *meaning "to move." Psychokinesis, telekinesis, and mind over matter all refer to the ability to move things, affect their physical properties, or determine the outcome of events by using the power of your mind. It works because thought triggers relatively large amounts of physical energy. Because we are connected to everything, this thought power can move or influence things. You need to be cautious regarding the energy you project so that it does not harm or inconvenience someone else. Psychokinesis, which can occur both spontaneously and deliberately, is independent of space and time.*

You can test your telekinetic powers by determining in advance the outcome of a coin toss. Write down your intended outcome for 50 coin tosses. Toss the coin and record the outcome. Did you do better than chance? Spoon bending is one of the more popular ways to demonstrate mind over matter. Some people, especially children, can easily affect utensils, probably because they still rely heavily on their intuitive brain and also because no one has ever told them that they can't bend a spoon!

The power of positive thinking should never be underestimated, especially when it comes to dealing with mind over matter. When you are on the road, project good weather

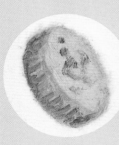

into the next day or city. Consciously clear obstacles from the road ahead. Use your power to cause a last-minute cancellation in a booked hotel so you can have a room. Delay the plane or train just a little bit so you can make your connection on time. Of course, you need to be aware of the potential consequences to other travelers and consider any inconvenience you might cause through your intentions. It is very important when you use this technique, as with all other psychic techniques, that as you open up to the powers of the intuitive process, you consciously desire the highest good to occur, which may sometimes result in missing your connection or not getting a room in the hotel that you desire.

The technique to accomplish these tasks has been described as relaxed attention. If you worry too much about whether the clouds will dissipate or the traffic will clear, you are bringing too much left-brain energy into the process, and what you want to happen never will. Movement or changes to physical things or events cannot be affected by mere wishes. It is a process of shifting from the analytic mind into the intuitive mind, which is the reverse of other intuitive processes. Once you have the vision of what you want to occur, you need to let go of the preoccupation with the event occurring and shift your mind to other things while your unconscious focuses on the task.

Test your telekinetic powers by determining in advance the outcome of a coin toss.

Remote Viewing

Remote viewing is the ability to describe or give details about a remote target, using your own style of intuition, without knowing anything about the target. This target can be a physical distance from you, can be shielded from you in some fashion, or may have existed in a past time. Remote viewers are able to describe a place that they have never visited. They can tell details about an event that happened years ago. They can describe what activities people might be doing in another part of the world. They can express images about an object that is locked in a box or in another room. In remote viewing, time and space are meaningless. This technique is also known as mental projection—projecting our minds into a different space or time. Remote viewing is a skill that has been claimed for centuries by wise men and women, or shamans, in Tibet, Siberia, Africa, and India.

The benefits of remote viewing when traveling are many. You will be able to spot traffic jams and change your route to avoid them. You will see that the perfect place to spend the night is just around the bend. Knowing the best place to vacation will make your leisure time even more enjoyable. Even before you book a room, you will sense the hospitality or know that you will feel relaxed in a particular hotel, guest house, or bed-and-breakfast. You will be able to find a hotel or attraction in an unfamiliar place. Knowing whether to take the train, bus, or taxi to your next location is important when you want to get somewhere quickly or safely or to find the best scenery. When you want the perfect local dining experience, you will be able to find the best restaurant in town.

Although the term *remote viewing* implies actually seeing an object, place, or person, all the senses are involved. You may see these objects, sense them, or hear information about them. You may have an impression about their taste or texture. It is not a meditative, dream, or trance state. During a remote viewing session, the viewer is always fully awake and alert.

Emanuel Swedenborg—an eighteenth-century Swedish scientist, inventor, and mystic— was well known for his remote visions. His vision of a spiritual world combined modern science and religion in a way that had not been explored before. Hypnotists in the eighteenth and early nineteenth centuries found that many of their subjects, while under hypnosis, could describe distant locations. Some could also see into other people's bodies to identify areas of disease. The term *remote viewing* was coined in 1971. The existence of Jupiter's rings was remote viewed in 1973 and later confirmed by space probes. It is now known that the CIA used remote viewers to help penetrate the Iron Curtain during the Cold War and for classified military projects. It is also used for criminal investigations,

Use your remote viewing skills to see the traffic jam ahead.

stock market predictions, and space exploration. The government has used remote viewing for years, yet our Western world is still struggling with concepts such as consciousness and intuition!

In the Western world, remote viewing has a higher status than other forms of paranormal events, such as the clairvoyant ability to pick cards or colors. Scientists are very interested in the ability of some people to remotely view geographic locations, hidden objects, archaeological sites, and objects in space. Obviously this information is very useful and could be obtained much more inexpensively than actually visiting a site or sending someone to a location. Research in clairvoyance, telepathy, and out-of-body all played a role in the development of remote viewing.

Psychic viewing is the ability to see remote objects such as geographic locations, hidden objects, and archaeological sites.

The difference between remote viewing and other clairvoyant and psychic phenomena is that there are strict science-based protocols for developing remote-viewing skills. Researchers developed a structured approach that allowed remote viewing to be highly teachable. It is based on observing the process of people with the innate skill. This approach was used to teach the military and is used as the basis for many of the remote-viewing techniques taught today. The researchers referred to the training as "expanding the parameters of perception" instead of "using psychic skills." The training centers teach the remote viewer to ignore distracting information and focus on one incoming stream of related information. Viewers are then taught how to access this information in their subconscious and bring it through to their conscious. The basic goal is to transfer intuitive information from the right brain into accessible analytic information in the left brain. Then this information can be translated into words, images, or sensations.

Practicing remote viewing offers general benefits to the exploring psychic. Your ability to more quickly induce altered states of consciousness will dramatically increase. You will significantly improve your ability to predict hidden images using psychometry. Your ability to travel in your mind to your chosen location in space-time will be greatly improved, and the accuracy of your imagery will be increased.

This, like other psychic skills, works because of the ability to tap into what Jung called the collective unconscious. Within this "place," all things, situations, and people are accessible because we are all connected and time and space are irrelevant.

However, like all of the techniques in this book, the ability to quiet your mind via meditation and trust in your innate skills is paramount. Perhaps the fact that the government has sanctioned the existence of this ability makes it easier for people to develop their skills because "proof" might serve to silence skeptical internal critics.

Practice: Learning Remote Viewing

It is necessary to have a target so that accuracy can be checked. If you have a friend who lives in another part of the world or even across town, you can remote view their activities at a certain time in the day. Focusing on a person that you know will help develop your skill, because there is already a connection between you and that person. Later you can move to places and objects with which you have no personal connection.

As you begin to get images in whatever intuitive mode works for you, verbalize them in a stream-of-conscious process. It is important to also record your feelings in words and sketches as you might capture the essence of something, or portions of the physicality of the place or object, that are easier to dissect in pictures than in words.

The basic steps are as follows:

✳ What is the overall nature of the site or target? Is it land, water, a building, or event?

✳ Use your senses to get impressions of sounds, colors, tastes, textures, and temperatures.

✳ What is your impression of the target's physical dimensions? How tall is it? How wide? Does it have angles or curves? Is it dense or transparent? You may begin to sketch your perceptions at this point as other images may come to you as you "see" the target.

✳ Try to get more detailed information. Note smaller features. What is the mood of the place? What's behind the image?

✳ Now that you have a strong connection with the target, question your intuition to see if there is anything you are missing. Ask which areas of the target need to be further explored.

✳ Continue to add to your sketch, and note any other qualitative information that comes to you.

Create a sketch of the remote object in order to capture important details and the essence of the place or object.

Energy of a Place

Why do some places feel right and uplifting and others feel unbalanced or even threatening? Feeling the energy of a place is a great skill when you are in unfamiliar surroundings. Energy expresses itself in vibrational frequencies. Quantum physics discovered that everything is compressed vibrating energy. Therefore we actually "feel" a place tangibly as well as intuitively.

There are many energy centers, power centers, or vortexes around the world that hold high concentrations of magnetic or electrical energy. Often they become the sites for chapels, temples, oracles, and cathedrals. Machu Picchu, the Great Pyramid of Giza, Stonehenge, Sedona (Arizona), and Denver (Colorado) are a few examples of where these energies come into special alignment.

This vortex energy is said to positively affect the chakra system, the acupuncture meridians, the endocrine system, and the pineal and pituitary glands, which assists in emotional release and increases psychic awareness.

Energy centers contain high concentrations of magnetic or electrical energy.

Our ancestors were able to feel the energy of many thousands of small sacred sites scattered across the earth. Their connection to the "Mother" or Mother Earth, was strong because they relied on her to supply their physical needs, cure their sicknesses, and balance their spirit.

Pathways around the earth, called *ley lines*, transmit and receive energy from place to place. Think of them like acupuncture meridians on the human body. The Australian Aboriginals identified pathways that connected the sacred sites of their land, which they called the Dreamings. Native cultures in the Americas called them Spirit Paths. These pathways in England connect many ancient sacred sites. The ancestors knew that the energy centers heightened their consciousness and made even deeper connections to their source.

Every person will react differently to an energy location, relating more to some than to others. There is no right way to feel about any one spot. You will receive the benefits from the energy of each center that is most suited to your needs at that time. Trust your intuition to be drawn to a place because it speaks deeply to you. Be receptive to messages.

Send your roots down into Mother Earth in order to reconnect with your intuitive self.

Feeling grounded helps you stay solidly in your body no matter what is going on around you. Like a root firmly latched into the soil, you aren't easily swept away but you can bend. When you are in this state, you are more aware of your environment and of the sensations and energy in your own body. This helps you to stay rooted in the present and appropriately respond to the world.

Practice: Grounding Exercise to Connect to the Earth's Energy

✳ Sit, stand, or lie down, whichever is most comfortable for you.

✳ Close your eyes and focus on your breath.

✳ Let your breath get deeper and deeper as you allow your body to sink into the chair or floor.

✳ As your breath continues to deepen, imagine a connection between you and the earth below you as if you had roots.

✳ Feel your roots going through the floor, into the soil, down into the rocks, way down into the bedrock, and ultimately into the core of the earth.

✳ Feel your strong connection with Mother Earth.

✳ You can now ask Mother Earth to send you healing, loving, grounding energy. Imagine it flowing up through your roots into your body. Feel the warmth as it spreads throughout your body.

✳ The more you practice this, the more quickly you will be able to ground yourself. To intensify the process, stand barefoot on the grass or earth and focus on your roots going down to the earth's core while receiving a flow of energy from the earth.

This skill can help you anytime you feel fear, worry, confusion, or hopelessness, bringing you back to a solid, calm center. You will then be able to see your situation more clearly and respond in an appropriate manner. This is very useful when you are traveling and become lost or confused, when it is late and you haven't found a place to stay, or when you are feeling threatened and you need the help of Mother Earth to reconnect you to your intuitive self so that you can make the best decision.

CHAPTER SEVEN *Let me sleep on it. How many times have you uttered that phrase or heard someone else say it and never given any thought to what it really meant? Dreams are storehouses of information and deep wells of creativity. They are a language we speak our entire lives, but may never really learn or pay attention to. Yet, dreams can be sources of inspiration for creating music, painting, and dance; provide insight to perplexing problems and clues to health or relationship problems; and provide nighttime practice for learning or improving skills.*

Your Dreams

Messages in dreams are usually presented symbolically. Data is presented in the language of metaphor, which the conscious dreamer then interprets upon awakening to make choices and decisions. The dream allows your conscious self to have a relationship with your deepest being, your *daimon*.

Almost all dreams provide an extremely valuable service to the dreamer. If we block them, we are probably missing their immediate benefit; if we remember but ignore them, we may be missing the vital message that they are trying to bring us about our life. If we deny or ignore our dream messages from the subconscious for too long, then they simply speak louder to get our attention, often by bringing related events into our waking hours. These events show up as sickness, accidents, relationship difficulties, and other unfortunate personal circumstances that force us outright to deal with the issue at hand.

The dream is incomplete without *dreamwork*—active interpretation of the dream followed by appropriate action. Dreamwork provides a way to channel the insights from your dream into your everyday life.

Dreams

"I do not believe that I am now dreaming but I cannot prove I am not," once mused Bertrand Russell, a twentieth-century English philosopher.

What do dreams do for us? Dreams let us fly, reconnect with loved ones, visit foreign lands, receive counsel from wise teachers, and receive personal messages about our future, jobs, relationships—anything that is important in fulfilling our unique mission. Dreams can shake us up, wake us up, and open us up to living life more fully.

In the ancient world, dreams were viewed as a source of divination—as prophetic. In ancient Greece, dreams were said to hold messages about healing, and people came to dream in temples to receive advice from priests and priestesses about the cures their dreams prophesied. Some cultures believe it is dangerous to wake someone lest their soul be lost, because during sleep, one's soul leaves his or her body to live in a special dream-world. In some Asian cultures, you can buy someone else's dream (a penny will do) if you think you need the message that it imparts.

My friend occasionally has dreams about people who she hasn't seen in a while who reappear in her life the next day. They may call her or she may bump into them on the street. They always have some information to tell her, some important reason that they needed to talk. Now when she gets one of her "nightly visits" she doesn't wait, but contacts the "visitor" first thing in the morning to see what is going on. This is another way of being conscious of your intuitive mode—the way you receive information. Instead of just getting an urge to call someone, she actually receives a visit in a dream—hard to ignore!

We spend about one-third of our lifetime in sleep. Dreams occur during sleep in a period called REM—rapid eye movement. There are four or five REM periods during the night, totaling about 1 1/2 hours and occurring every

90 to 100 minutes. Each successive period gets longer so that the later REM sessions may last up to 40 minutes. These periods contain the dreams that are the most vivid and most often remembered. Reports of morning dreams are typically richer and more complex than those collected early at night. We are not the only ones who dream—as dream states have been observed in many mammals, including dogs, monkeys, elephants, rats, and possums.

Nightmares are just as important to pay attention to as pleasant dreams, perhaps more so. A nightmare is an elaborate, intense dream characterized by vivid, visual imagery and strong negative feelings, such as intense fear, anxiety, or guilt.

More nightmares are reported during periods of stress, such as illness, job and lifestyle changes, or the loss of a person important to the dreamer. A reduction or discontinuance of nightmares is common when the sufferer feels more confident and in control of their situation and less attached to the helpless feelings of childhood.

Nightmares are just as important to pay attention to as pleasant dreams, perhaps even more so.

Nightmares play the role of jolting the dreamer into receiving information that would be difficult for them to accept in a conscious state. Carl Jung observed that when we disown our shadow sides, they are projected outward into dreams as monsters, natural disasters, or intimidating beings. The nightmare helps people become aware of these lost or unwanted parts of themselves so they can accept them back into the psyche.

Nightmares provide a valuable service by offering dreamers a needed emotional release. If you ignore or block them, you will miss the personal message that may be critical to your life. However, if you act upon the insight that the dream is trying to impart, you may be able to avoid additional terrifying dreams as well as implement an early cure for the situation that is disturbing you.

Recalling Dreams

Have you ever awakened in the middle of the night after a wonderful dream and told yourself that you would remember it upon awakening? Me, too. In the morning, it is lost. You may remember that you had a dream, or perhaps even pieces of it, but never enough to analyze. Make a conscious decision to plan to remember whatever dreams come to you. As you honor your dreams and record them, you will recall them more easily. It is as if the dreamworld knows you are taking it seriously and will be more forthcoming with the messages and in cooperating with your memory during dream recall.

Inspirational Dreams

There are numerous instances of musical compositions, inventions, poetry, and paintings that were inspired by a dream. The Beatles' song "Yesterday," Samuel Taylor Coleridge's poem "Kubla Khan," and Robert Louis Stevenson's *The Strange Case of Dr. Jekyll and Mr. Hyde* have been attributed to dreams. Coleridge says that he fell asleep while reading about that Mongol conqueror and awoke to write down a fully developed poem he seemed to have composed while dreaming. Many artists—including Mozart, Beethoven, William Blake, Paul Klee, Ingmar Bergman, and Sting—credit their dreams as a source of inspiration.

Thomas Edison attributes many of his inventions to dreams. Friedrich Kekulé discovered the structure of the benzene ring after he saw a snake swallowing its tail in a dream. Elias Howe dreamed a solution to a problem that perplexed him as he struggled with the construction of the sewing machine. Stories say that he fell asleep at his workbench and dreamed of cannibals poking at him with spears containing holes in their points. Upon awakening, he realized that the trick to making his sewing machine work was to move the hole to the point of the needle.

Practice: Recalling Your Dreams

Here are some suggestions for recalling your dreams:

❋ Keep some writing paper and a pen by your bed for your dream diary.

❋ In the morning, stay still and try to recall if you had any dreams. Move gently into various sleep positions; stop between each one to see if you have any recall in those positions.

❋ Initially recall your dreams with your eyes closed; opening them will affect recall.

❋ Your dreams may come to you later in the day or even several days later. Always take the time to record them.

❋ If you are having trouble remembering any dreams, you could set an alarm to wake up at 90-minute intervals to catch your dreams. You will have a better chance of catching dreams in the morning.

❋ Add titles to your dreams. It will help you to recall them later and trigger patterns among your dream messages.

❋ Date your dream entries so that you can connect the dream with the time line of events in your life.

❋ Be sure to capture the details of your dream—ask yourself questions about where you were, what was around you, whether there were any unusual sounds or smells. In what order did the events happen? Note any associations or interpretations that come to you.

❋ Sometimes a simple picture or diagram helps to bring to life details or certain aspects of the dream that are more easily shown in a picture.

To catch your dreams, use an alarm clock to wake you during the night.

Dream Interpretation and Dreamwork

All dreams need dreamwork. If we ignore our dreams, the messages they are trying to give us will come through stronger and more forceful in our waking life or in our dream life. Therefore we owe it to ourselves to be aware of these messages and take appropriate action to use these insights in our daily life.

There are many approaches to dream interpretation. Some dream interpretations look at universal symbols. Others believe that every character and object in the dream is actually one component of the dreamer, so the dreamer needs to look at the dream from all angles. Freud believed that a dreamer should associate separately with each element in the dream, because each element would have a personal meaning for the dreamer. Many analysts believe that the dream should be interpreted as a whole, as a symbolic representation of the dreamer's current situation or state of mind.

The dream image of riding on a dolphin can be interpreted in many ways and may be highly personal to the dreamer.

Dreamwork could include reflecting on the symbols or images presented during the dream, having a dialogue with a dream figure using stream-of-consciousness writing (described in Chapter Two), intuitively bringing an unfinished dream to resolution perhaps by using a pendulum or other tool, and creating art to bring the dream images to life and see what else arises.

The emotion experienced in the dream is important to identify in order to interpret the symbols accurately. Consider your emotion during the dream—terrified, guilty, resentful, happy, confused—as well as the residue emotion after waking. If you can identify the emotion within a dream or upon wakening, it may help you to identify the area in your life that needs attention.

The creation of a mandala is just one form of dreamwork; find the method that works best for you.

The act of drawing, painting, or sculpting dream images may make the relationship between the dream objects clearer and reveal hidden connections. Dreams continue to unfold their meaning as they come to life via art. The surrealists used a technique called automatism, in which they painted without stopping to analyze the forthcoming images. Much of the surrealist art was a representation of the dream world.

I have found that drawing images using the context of a mandala helps me to identify the underlying meaning of the dream. Mandalas are used by many spiritual traditions for healing and transformation. The process of making any type of sacred art stimulates deep insights about our inner or higher self. It can express contradictory information in a way that can be grasped and integrated. It can show us that our existence and the universe are connected, thus allowing us to understand things in a more inclusive and holistic way.

Practice: Learning Dreamwork

There are many, many ways to work with your dreams. Here are some suggestions for working with different aspects of your dream. Different dreams may require different types of dreamwork.

✳ What is the meaning of the dream's setting? Is it in a small, secret place, a cavernous space, or a familiar space?

✳ What are the dream images? Are they colorful, or do they lack color? What energy, or lack of energy, does the image hold?

✳ Is there a common theme to the dream? What would its title be?

✳ Are there events or movements? Does it represent a shift of energy or attitude?

✳ What are your emotions during the dream and upon waking? Are they different?

✳ What is going on in your life? The past few days? Have you been seeking a solution to a problem?

✳ Is the dream similar to other dreams you've had or to famous stories or legends?

✳ Could the dream be showing your shadow side—a side you would rather not acknowledge?

✳ Relive the dream either through meditation or stream-of-consciousness writing to dialogue with the characters.

✳ Imagine that you are one of the dream characters. Perhaps create a mask or draw a picture of this character to embody the energy and inner reality of that character.

✳ Draw, paint, or sculpt the images. As images take shape, deeper meanings will unfold.

✳ Is the dream an answer to a current question or problem, a comment on your current situation, a warning about some decision or action?

✳ How did the dream end? How would you have preferred it to end?

✳ Are archetypal images or universal symbols present—such as the Great Mother, the Hero, the Wise Old Man/Woman, the Lover, the Warrior?

✳ Finally, act on the dream—make a decision, answer a question, or do something to keep communication with the dream world open and active.

Use Your Dream Time—Incubate Your Dreams

You can ask your dreams anything. Because you are the source of all information and have all the answers, all you have to do is ask. Do you want to know how to solve a problem with your business or a relationship? Are you stuck and can't come up with new ideas for a course you are teaching? Are you concerned about a particular health problem? Do you want to know whether switching jobs and relocating is a good idea? You will get answers—perhaps some will be direct and obvious, whereas others will require interpretation. Dream incubation is easily learned, and the benefits are priceless!

Practice: Incubating Dreams

✳ Choose a night when you are not overtired and will have enough time in the morning to record your dream.

✳ Before going to sleep, record in your journal the emotions you experienced during the day.

✳ Write briefly about the issue you would like to dream about.

✳ Formulate a clear, succinct question or request, in one line, that states what you would like to understand or what you need. This will clear your mind of other issues and focus your intention. Similar to working with the pendulum, the statement should not be ambiguous.

✳ Repeat your one-line incubation phrase over and over as you fall asleep.

✳ Whenever you awaken, either in the morning or in the middle of the night, write down what you were thinking or dreaming. You may need some time to explore the metaphors and interpret the dream. However, dream incubation is so powerful that many people find their answers come to them quite clearly, sometimes in the form of songs playing through their minds.

Lucid Dreams

In a lucid dream, you are aware that you are dreaming and can sometimes move around in the dream of your own volition. You might even alter some or all aspects of the dream as the dream is occurring. You can use lucid dreams to ask questions, stand up to monsters, or learn or practice a skill. Researchers believe that children are actually practicing how to talk, walk, and do other skills while they are sleeping. Paul Tholey, a psychologist and lucid-dream researcher who worked in the late twentieth century, had great success using dreamwork in his training of the German Olympic ski jumping team. He taught the skiers lucid-dreaming techniques so that they could practice and experiment with new maneuvers without risk of injury.

Practice: Lucid Dreaming

❉ First, increase dream recall as explained previously.

❉ Get up 1½ to 3 hours before your normal waking hour. Be sure to be completely awake for 30 to 90 minutes. Return to sleep. Alternatively take a morning nap. Because we have more REM activity in the morning, the chance of a lucid dream increases.

❉ When you wake up, recall as many dreams as possible. Before you go back to sleep, tell yourself that the next time you are dreaming, you will know that you are dreaming. Imagine going back into the dream you just had as you fall asleep and perform some planned activity.

❉ As you go to bed, be confident that you will have a lucid dream. Know what activity you will try, such as flying, if you find yourself in the middle of a lucid dream.

Astral Travel

Astral travel is more commonly known as an out-of-body experience. It is the ability to leave your physical body and travel anywhere throughout space. Out-of-body experiences often occur while resting or when trying to sleep. These astral dreams are vivid and the experience does not fade, rather like real events. It is similar to lucid dreaming in that you consciously try to control what is happening.

Out-of-body experiences can teach us that we are more than our physical beings. It can help us to perceive a greater reality; decrease fear and anxiety around death; enhance psychic abilities, such as precognition and telepathy; and induce spontaneous healing.

I believe that the most important effect all these skills and activities produce, whether we need the adventure of an out-of-body experience or are content to interpret our dreams, is a stronger connection to our spiritual essence and greater confidence in our ability to know how to obtain the answers we seek.

During astral travel, we leave our physical body and travel anywhere throughout space.

CHAPTER EIGHT *I do not believe that the future is predetermined. We have the ability at every turn to make our own decision about which direction to pursue. Being able to tune into our psychic abilities—or better yet, be constantly plugged in—gives us the added advantage of knowing what is best for us every step of the way.*

Seeing Your Future

When you tap into that infinite realm, or the collective unconscious, you may see potential crisis in addition to positive opportunities. If you have a warning premonition, the event can be altered or avoided or, at the very least, you can be better prepared. The effect of accidents can be minimized if you are on high alert. Business deals gone bad or an unavoidable setback can be dealt with in the least traumatic way. Even if you believe that a loved one will soon die, this extra time will give you the opportunity to spend more time with them—time that you can both cherish.

A good friend of mine was recently trying to make a decision about whether to return to North Carolina after relocating to Maine because of her husband's health problems. One day she suddenly felt the urge to call a friend from North Carolina with whom she had not spoken in a long time. As the conversation unfolded, my friend found out that her friend was in the process of renovating a cottage to rent. My friend was overjoyed at finding a place to stay for as long as she wanted while deciding whether to move back to North Carolina permanently.

Acting on hunches often sets up synchronistic events that can assist you in moving forward in your life. I don't know what the future holds for my friend—nor does she, I am sure—but I know she will continue to rely on her intuition to guide her.

Visualization

Visualization is similar to dream incubation in that we enter the state with a particular intention or question and then wait to receive images, voices, or feelings that we can interpret and make sense of for our own lives. With this technique, you follow step-by-step instructions that lead you through a series of experiences to reach your source of wisdom. It is there that you can ask your questions and wait to receive guidance.

Visualization is commonly done in a group setting, led by a trained counselor who controls the sequence and timing of the journey and who can help you make sense of the messages. Alternatively, you can record a process that you play to yourself or memorize your steps in the journey.

Visualization is a good technique to use when you are faced with an important decision or when you feel there is something inside of you that needs to reveal itself with clues for your potential or next step. You may also find clues to dormant skills and areas of interest similar to the information you get from the dreamworld. Indeed, all of the techniques and processes presented in this book are accessing the same well of information—the place where all the answers lie. It is just a matter of finding the one that works best for you in the different situations throughout your life.

It is important to note that visualization is a conscious process in which you deliberately create imaginary scenes. When you first begin the process, it is difficult to distinguish which images are springing up from your intuitive mind—and therefore need to be paid attention to—and which are merely fantasy, fear, or desire. You can identify a psychic vision because you have a lack of control over shaping its image. As with the other intuitive processes, the messages you receive need to be correctly interpreted by relying on both your analytic skills and the wisdom of past experiences.

Practice: Learning Visualization

Decide whether you want to record your own process, memorize the steps into your visualization, or play a prerecorded tape of a journey that you like.

✳ Sit or lie down. Get comfortable, and close your eyes. You may want to do some alternate-nostril breathing or just take some deep breaths to relax.

✳ Imagine yourself beginning on a journey. You may decide to walk, take a train, fly, or go by boat. Picture the scenery that you are passing. What does the air smell like? Is it cold or warm? What do you see? Are the birds chirping or do you hear the wind rustling through the trees? Try to involve as many senses as possible.

✳ Arrive at your destination feeling refreshed and alert after your journey. You could be in a forest, on a beach, or on another planet.

✳ It is here that you will find a special place to ask your questions. This special place should feel sacred to you— perhaps a grotto of ancient trees, a small cave, or a beautiful soaring temple. Inside this sacred place is an altar, a stone, a person, or whatever feels right to you, which is the source of all wisdom.

✳ Ask your question of this source. Let whatever message, image, voice, or feeling you have arise in response to your question. You may get a glimpse, or a flash, or even something that seems completely inappropriate. Whatever it is, thank the source for your answer.

✳ Slowly return to your starting place, retracing all the steps of your journey.

Find a special place to ask your questions and wait to receive guidance.

Precognitive Dreams

Two weeks before his assassination, Abraham Lincoln had a dream that there was a funeral at the White House. "Who is in the casket?" he asked a soldier in the dream. The reply was, "the president of the United States." Many people have similar dreams before catastrophic events take place, about what will unfold. Many people had dreams of planes crashing and buildings collapsing before the attack on the World Trade Center in 2001. The breakup of the space shuttle Columbia *upon reentry also induced many precognitive dreams. A number of people canceled their bookings for the* Titanic *because of their dreams. Edgar Cayce predicted the stock market crash months before it occurred and foresaw the outbreak of World War II.*

Dreams that predict the future are called precognitive. They are usually vivid and fairly literal. Precognitive dreams might help explain the feeling of déjà vu. This is the experience in which you feel that you have been in the same situation before, to the extent that you know what will happen next or what your friend will say next. Many of our dreams foreshadow future events. We may forget the dream yet experience the remembering through déjà vu.

Many precognitive dreams are simple warnings that certain events might occur unless an action is taken, guidance to be alert to a certain situation, or clues to personal issues that need attention. You have a choice to heed the message in your dreams or not. For example, if you dream about the brakes failing on your car causing you to get into an accident, you can choose to get your brakes tested and repaired if necessary. Your dream could also mean that you need to slow down in general and examine your daily routine. Dreams about future illnesses are helpful to bring awareness to symptoms that are not yet available to consciousness.

Practice: Precognitive Dreaming

✳ Follow the instructions for dream incubation in Chapter Sevem. Focus on future events that you are considering taking part in—for example, a future relationship, travel plans, a new job, buying a house, returning to school.

✳ You can also incubate a dream about your health, asking for clues to potential problems.

✳ It is important to record your dreams so you can look for connections between your waking life and dreaming life. In the evening or at a convenient time, read your dream journal from the past few days and reflect on the events of your day. An event portended in a precognitive dream usually occurs within two days. This active association of dreams to events will help you be more aware of your style of precognitive dream and more able to recognize them in advance.

Many precognitive dreams are frightening. Some traditional cultures symbolically reenact the event in a minor way with the intention of preventing its serious occurrence. However, having these dreams in advance of the event gives you time to prepare so you can gather your strength and be alert to the warning signs. Therefore it is possible to recognize the pattern in waking life soon enough to avoid the catastrophe. These dreams help us pay attention to the seemingly insignificant details that we often overlook. The cultivation of these dreams can be beneficial to ourselves as well as to the people we dream about.

Our dreams often foreshadow future events—many cancelled bookings on the Titanic due to their dreams.

Runes

The rune is not only a letter in an old Germanic alphabet but also a sacred concept or idea similar to arcane in the tarot. Similar to tarot cards, runes are an oracle from which you seek advice. The word rune *means "whisper" or "secret." The runes had religious or magical significance for the people who wrote them. Each one has phonetic pronunciation, can be translated into a phrase, and has a sound associated with it and a physical posture to represent it. It is an entire story of a relationship to a Norse God and is full of meanings that represent the forces of nature and the mind.*

Runes are still around us today—the peace symbol is a form of the Yr-rune of the Younger Futhark. Dutch "hex signs," so common on barns, are also derived from a runic source. Even the wood used in construction in old Germanic buildings incorporated the shape of the rune so that the runic power would be passed on to the building's inhabitants.

The old Germanic Runic alphabet, or "Elder Futhark," contains 24 runes. Today, you are able to buy a pouch of rune stones, which are identical pieces of wood or stone into which the rune symbols are cut.

Runic divination is called runecasting. When your unconscious mind focuses on your question, selecting a rune stone is a synchronistic event. It is not "you" randomly picking the stone, but your intuition deliberately selecting a particular stone. In fact, the same question will usually produce similar responses from both the runes and the tarot. I believe we lean more toward one oracle than the other because of our cultural or environmental background.

A rune reading will look at a particular issue from the past, present, and future. It addresses the concern of what will happen if we follow our current path. In that, it is a valuable predictor not of the future, per se, but of the possibility of a particular outcome.

The Meanings of the Runes

F-ehu (cattle/mobile property)—The essence of money and the power needed to attain personal material wealth.

U-ruz (the aurochs/ox)—Symbolizes strength, vitality, and good personal health.

Th-urisaz (the strong one/giant)—Symbolizes regeneration and destruction.

A-nsuz (ancestral god)—The essence of spiritual power and numinous knowledge.

R-aidho (wagon/chariot)—Represents the mystery of divine and natural law, the laws of cause and effect.

K-enaz (torch)—Symbolizes the ability to generate and create.

G-ebo (gift/generosity)—Represents all aspects of giving and ecstasy.

W-unjo (joy/delight)—Related to harmonious existence and relationship of all things.

H-agalaz (hailstone)—The number 9 is the most sacred number; this rune defines the framework of the universe as complete and harmonious.

N-audhiz (need)—Symbolizes distress and deliverance from that distress.

I-sa (ice)—Contains the mystery of the black hole and stillness.

J-era (harvest/good season)—Represents the cyclical pattern of the universe.

Ei-hwaz (yew tree/tree of life)—Symbolizes the mystery of life and death, eternal life and endurance.

P-erthro (dice cup used for casting lots)—Represents the concept of past action affecting the present; synchronicity.

Eiha-z (elk)—Symbolizes a protective force and a connection between gods and men.

S-owilo (sun)—Represents the spiritual force that guides one on his or her path.

T-iwaz (the god Tyr)—Represents law and justice.

 B-erkano (birch goddess)— Represents the mystery of the earth mother and the birth-life-death-rebirth cycle.

 E-hwaz (horse)—Symbolizes the harmonious relationship between two forces—trust and loyalty.

 M-annaz (human)—Represents the mystery of the divine in every person.

 L-aguz (water)—Represents the potential of life and the passage to and from life.

 Ing-waz (the god Ing)—An earth god representing potential energy or gestation.

 D-agaz (day)—Symbolizes total awakening.

 O-thala (property/homeland)— The essence of a sacred enclosure, and material and spiritual power inherited from the ancestors.

A rune reading gives a suggestion about how to understand your current situation and a likely outcome if nothing changes. Rune lore acknowledges that the future is not fixed and depends upon your actions. However, the readings are sometimes cryptic and thus not easily understood. It takes a long time to properly interpret runecastings. You need to proceed with caution because the runes are very comprehensive and perhaps only one part of a particular rune's meaning applies to your situation. Your intuition is key to figuring out the underlying meaning of the message and your interpretation of the possible outcomes will enable you to consider all of the possibilities.

Practice: How to Do a Runecasting

Runecasting is the act of formulating a question in your mind and then allowing your intuitive mind to pick one or more runes from a bag or container and cast them onto a surface. Traditionally, a white cloth was using for working with the runes, which forms a boundary for the casting.

You can make your own runes by painting the 24 rune symbols on pieces of stone or wood, or you can buy a set. There are numerous ways to cast the runes, including many formal procedures, but you can make up your own or use any of the layouts used for tarot readings.

✳ For daily inspiration, or as a focus for your attention throughout your day, pick one rune from your bag. Meditate on its meaning for a few minutes. Notice what happens during the day that was predicted by the rune.

✳ Perform a Norns cast—the Norns are the Norse goddesses of fate. Pick three runes from your bag, focusing on a particular situation. The first rune provides insight into the past, the second indicates the path that you are currently on, and the third represents the future outcome if you continue on the same path.

✳ Reach into your bag and intuitively select nine runes; nine is a magical number in Germanic mythology. Cast the runes onto your cloth. Those that land in the center of your cloth and that are faceup contain the most pertinent insights into your situation. The farther away from the center the runes are, the less relevant they are to figuring out your issue, or they may suggest general influences. The runes that are facedown represent outside or future influences.

Runes can be used in many ways—as a daily inspiration or to provide clarity for a particular situation or question.

Vision Mirrors

The image of a gypsy fortune-teller gazing into her crystal ball to predict your future is a popular misconception of the power of scrying. This divination art dates back to the ancient Egyptians and Arabs and was brought into the public eye via Nostradamus's use of a bowl of water to prophesy the future. Scrying can be used to answer questions, find lost objects or people, help solve crimes, and get glimpses of the future. Characters in many fairy tales and legends, such as the Wizard of Oz *and the* Lord of the Rings, *have used crystal balls to locate their adversaries.*

Scrying works by reducing sensory inputs, which helps you to approach an altered state of consciousness. If you have ever stared at a blank wall or at the ceiling on a sleepless night until you began to hallucinate and see images or figures, you have experienced this state. This state has been called the *ganzfeld*, which is German for "all field." By staring into an unobstructed, featureless field of light, researchers in the 1930s found that people were able to enter an altered state. Their attention was turned inward more quickly than with traditional meditation practices.

The reflective surface of a scrying device accomplishes the same thing by reducing visual distractions and freeing the mind to go inward. Any reflective object or surface—such as a mirror, a shiny stone, or a bowl of water—can be used to access information through visions.

The most important aspect of scrying—as with every other divination tool or psychic skill—is accurately interpreting what you are seeing by relying on both your analytical skills and your past experiences, as well as entering the exercise with the highest intentions. The images that are revealed to you can be interpreted in ways similar to the images from your dreams or visualizations.

Practice: Scrying

✳ Fill a shallow dish with water. Add black food coloring so the surface is reflective.

✳ Set candles around the room so that their reflection can be seen in the water but are not in your direct line of vision.

✳ Sit comfortably in front of your scrying surface. You do not want to be able to see your reflection in the water, so you should be looking at the bowl from an angle.

✳ Breathe deeply as you gaze at the water. You may want to start with alternate-nostril breathing to stimulate both sides of your brain.

✳ You will need to meditate on the water for at least 10 minutes, but more preferably 30 minutes. While you are meditating, focus on receiving information from your deities or higher self that is for the highest good of all involved.

✳ Your eyes should be unfocused so that your vision is slightly blurry and not directly fixed on anything.

✳ Relax and allow images to come up either on the surface of the water or through voices or feelings.

When you have finished, write down all the images that you received, no matter how small or strange. Use your intuitive and analytic skills to interpret what they mean for you.

Scrying can be used to answer questions, find lost objects or people, and also to get glimpses of the future.

Conclusion: You Have the Power!

I hope this book has opened your eyes and increased your awareness of the psychic skills that lie within you. Perhaps you will now start to trust and make use of the whole assortment of intuitive abilities that you were born with and use them to make your life flow more smoothly. Believing in and tapping into the vast realm of information—the collective unconscious—will enrich and deepen your everyday experiences. Have the confidence to use these skills in all aspects of your life, from home and work to health and travel. I believe that you will experience a sense of peace coming from this newfound source of inner strength and belief in yourself as you connect with your path and find clues to your potential.

In this increasingly complex world, we need to be able to use our entire mind—both the analytic side and the intuitive side—to make the very best decisions about the present and the future as we possibly can.

We need to challenge the Western concept that analytic intelligence is more important than intuition. Excessive logic and rational thinking only serve to cut us off from our complete power by not giving any voice to our intuitive intelligence. By opening your intuitive channel, this higher level of awareness will allow you to recognize the more insignificant distractions and problems of everyday life and treat them as minor issues.

You can do your part as a manager or a coworker by giving the same weight to someone's gut feeling as a carefully prepared spreadsheet. At home, you can encourage the use of intuition in your children by talking with them about their dreams, playing guessing games, and really listening to them when they say they don't like someone. Treat your spouse or partner and friends with respect when they share their perceptions, dream images, and stories of synchronicities with you.

Consider making meditation a part of your morning or evening routine to bring both sides of your mind into balance, creating an optimal state for opening to intuitive insights. Be childlike and trust that your intuition has all the answers you need. Pay attention to images and feelings that arise in those moments before you fully wake up and when you are drifting off to sleep. Take the time to be creative in whatever way your inner artist is struggling to express itself—whether through dance, art, gardening, chanting, running, meditation, or drumming.

Explore the exercises presented in this book to find out the best methods for you to lend support to your innate intuition. It may be one of the divination tools, dream interpretation, or incubation. You may find that you have a special talent for telepathy, remote viewing, or psychokinesis. Practicing positive imagery and believing in our bodies' own healing instincts are two very important areas that contribute to developing confidence and trust in our innate abilities. Remember that you have a unique way of receiving information, whether through images, sounds, voices, feelings, body sensations, or a knowing. Honor the method and take the time to learn your psychic language.

When it comes to intuition, trust yourself because you have the power!

Believing in and tapping into the source of all information will enrich and deepen your everyday experiences.

Index